Pulp Writer

Twenty Years in the
American Grub Street

PAUL S. POWERS

Edited and with biographical essays by Laurie Powers

University of Nebraska Press | Lincoln and London

Library of Congress Cataloging-in-Publication Data
Powers, Paul S. (Paul Sylvester), 1905–1971.
Pulp writer : twenty years in the American Grub
Street / Paul S. Powers ; edited and with biographical
essays by Laurie Powers. p. cm.
Includes bibliographical references (p.   ) and index.
ISBN-13: 978-0-8032-5984-3 (pbk. : alk. paper)
ISBN-10: 0-8032-5984-0 (pbk. : alk. paper)
1. Powers, Paul S. (Paul Sylvester), 1905–1971.
2. Authors, American—20th century—Biography.
3. Pulp literature—Authorship.   4. Western stories—
Authorship.   I. Powers, Laurie, 1957–   II. Title.
PS3531.O9725Z46   2007   813'.52—dc22
2006026244

Set in New Baskerville by Bob Reitz.
Designed by A. Shahan.

To Ruth Easton and Patricia Binkley

The quick beat of hoofs died into abrupt silence as
Sonny Tabor reined up his paint pony and came
to a halt. For several minutes the horseman loomed
against the lonely, star-haunted night.

"Steady, Paint," whispered the rider in a cool voice.
"There's a light down there. A ranch house, I reckon.
Wonder what it means this time—a job, or trouble?"

Paul S. Powers, *Wanted—Sonny Tabor* (1931)

CONTENTS

ILLUSTRATIONS

A NOTE ON THE TEXT

The memoir *Pulp Writer: Twenty Years in the American Grub Street* is not dated. Judging from the content and other correspondence, it appears to have been written in 1943.

PULP WRITER

Discovering *Pulp Writer*

1. (*preceding page*) Paul Powers and his cocker spaniel,
Mike, ca. 1951. *Author's collection.*

2. (*above*) The Powers girls, ca. 1962. *From left:* Patty,
Becky, Laurie, and Linda. *Author's collection.*

One day in June 1999, I drove to Garden Grove, California, to visit an aunt I hadn't seen in thirty-five years. She had some papers for me, she said: two boxes of personal papers that had belonged to my grandfather.

When I arrived, two blue plastic containers were perched on her kitchen table. They were those sturdy plastic numbers you can find at any hardware store, the perfect size for packing and storing items that are difficult to pack: old blankets, power tools, outgrown toys. Or, in this case, what was left of Grandpa's life. Sixty-six years of life shoved into two Easy Totes.

Pat assigned herself to one box, and I took command of the other. We cautiously opened them, and the musty smell of old paper drifted out. The boxes were packed to the brim with heaps of crumbling and fragile papers thrown in haphazardly. A disheveled mess.

"I just haven't had time to go through this stuff," Pat said. She gazed at her pile. She had a serenity and an overall air of bemusement that I assumed she inherited from her mother. From what I'd heard about my grandfather over the years, I couldn't imagine him possessing such mildness.

I looked at my box. This would take weeks, not hours.

Pat had mentioned in an earlier phone conversation that she thought her father had written a memoir, but she wasn't sure.

Careful, I thought. Don't get your hopes up. This might be nothing but junk.

Finding these documents was the culmination of ten months of investigating, interviewing, and traveling from Massachusetts, to Arizona, and finally to California to discover my real grandfather, rather than the image I'd had of him for most of my life. This image was like an old film reel stuck in a projector in my mind, unable to move beyond a few poorly-lit pictures that summed up his identity into exactly two categories. He was an alcoholic, a binge drinker who terrorized his family and disappeared from our lives when I was a little girl, leaving behind a memory full of confusion and contempt. But he was also a writer, an attribute that had always tempered my somewhat hostile memory of him. Yes, he was a drunk, but he had written a *novel.* It was, as I thought of it for most of my life, a silly little Western that was not a bestseller. But it had been *published.* Which was more than I, forty-two years old and still an unpublished writer, had accomplished. I'd always been slightly envious of my grandfather for that.

There are good reasons why my memory of my grandfather is so one-dimensional. Until a few years ago, the basic facts I knew about him made up a very short list. Some were drawn from sparse stories told by my mother and sisters. The rest were gleaned from the few documents, such as his death certificate, that I had collected over the years. Paul Sylvester Powers. My paternal grandfather. Known simply as Grandpa, not Grandpa Paul or Grandpa Powers. Born in 1905 in Little River, Kansas. Died in 1971 in Berkeley. His father was a physician. Fathered three children of his own: my father, John; a younger son, Tom; and a daughter, Pat. His novel *Doc Dillahay* was published in 1949. It didn't sell well. I didn't read the book until I was thirty-seven; when I did get around to reading it, it struck me as being a pleasant yet unimpressive story with snappy dialogue and a typical Western ending. And all of the characters grinned—all the time.

Grandpa's physical appearance is best portrayed by the portrait on the back of the *Doc Dillahay* dust jacket. Grandpa looks intellectual and intimidating in a wide-lapel suit, a broad chest, silvery hair just starting to recede. He wears glasses and looks stiffly off into the distance. He looks somewhat like Teddy Roosevelt, but without the toothy grin. I don't remember seeing my grandfather smile in any photograph.

I don't remember his looks at all, only where he worked and lived, which was a dark and dingy bookstore in Berkeley with new, used, disheveled, and stacked-to-the-ceiling books. An apartment somewhere. Light streaming through a window into an otherwise dreary room. I don't remember his face, what he said, what he did. I do remember a vague presence sitting in a chair next to the door like a sentry, saying good-bye. I was afraid of him; he was a stranger and hadn't really tried to talk to me that day. There was a feeling of suffocation in the apartment, and a sense of, well, failure.

When I was young, my sisters or my mother told me that he wrote what I thought were called "dime-store Westerns" under the pseudonym Ward Stevens. My mother mentioned when I was young that he wrote for obscure Western magazines. She didn't offer any more information, and I had the impression that the Western magazines hadn't amounted to much, so I assumed that what he wrote for them was insignificant. Where he lived while he dabbled in these frivolous endeavors, I had no idea.

When I was six or seven, I was cleaning out the bedroom I shared with my sister Becky. Crawling through piles of broken toys, plastic horses, and well-worn copies of *King of the Wind* and *Ramona*, I found a book—nothing new to me, since we had a lot of books scattered about the house, but this one was different. It was so small that it fit in the palm of my hand. The cover was cardboard, the illustration a crude watercolor of a cowboy on a galloping horse. The title, *Spook Riders on the Overland*, was emblazoned across the front, and the binding was crumbling so much that the whole sorry thing was held together with a rubber band. Ward M. Stevens was the author. "That's Grandpa," my sister told me. "He wrote it." But why was it so small, I wondered, and why didn't he use his real name?

During the 1960s, Grandpa and his second wife, Mary, worked at a used bookstore in Berkeley. My mother, my sisters, and I lived about thirty miles east in the small town of Livermore. Despite being home to the atomic-age Lawrence Radiation Laboratory and quickly growing with tract homes, Livermore was still a country town. I could walk to school and pass by the occasional farmhouse huddled in the middle of a block, peek through a hole in the fence and see the chicken coops and the weed-infested side yard, and feel the crunch of peppercorns fallen from the huge pepper trees rooted in front yards.

A bucolic setting, but one always blanketed by an unexplained layer of absence. My father, Grandpa's firstborn, had earned a Bronze Star in World War II and then had graduated with honors from the University of California, Berkeley and the University of California Medical School at San Francisco. But something tripped up afterward. Jack started to drink heavily during medical school. He and my mother divorced in 1958, a year after I was born. He drifted in and out of our lives afterward, marrying three more women but always managing to look homeless whenever he appeared at our front door. From 1960 to 1964 his life was a cycle of drinking, checking into sanitariums, drying out, and checking out—only to have it start all over again.

In 1964 my father died from cirrhosis; his liver was already weakened by hepatitis contracted from a patient years before, and the drinking accelerated his demise. He was thirty-nine years old. His death was the beginning of the disappearance of the rest of the Powers family.

My mother tried to keep in touch with Grandpa and Mary for a while, and we trooped over to Berkeley to visit them—at least once—and Grandpa loyally drove out to visit us during that period. But my mother remarried, and my stepfather didn't particularly care much for any of the Powers clan, especially my grandfather. Five years after my father's death, my family had shrunk from a family consisting of my mother's and father's families, totaling roughly twenty-five people, to only six: my mother, my stepfather, my three sisters, and myself. An island unto ourselves.

Occasionally the topic of Grandpa would arise, but I never had the courage to ask the hard questions. Instead, I waited for my sisters or my mother to volunteer information. Linda, the oldest, knew more about the family than the rest of us, and her memory eventually became the authoritative voice for my family history. Sometimes Grandpa would come up in conversation, and only then would I learn about him. He had a full sister, Nell; a half brother, George; and a half sister, Phyllis. With Mary, his second wife, he had two children: a son named Tom and a daughter named Pat. *I had an aunt and an uncle somewhere. I had cousins.* I hung onto these pieces of information as if I were holding small jewels in my hand.

Linda framed a newspaper article that ran in the *Orange County Register* that announced the publication of *Doc Dillahay* and hung it on a wall in her family room. Over the years I surreptitiously peered at the print. As I read the article, Grandpa's world seemed as distant and foreign as a celebrity's. I never read it completely; the pain was too great, and I was felt a little embarrassed by my curiosity. My sisters seemed to have moved on. Why couldn't I?

If I had read it, I would have found information about my grandfather that took me another twenty years to find.

My sisters coped, moved out of the house, got jobs, and got married. I had a harder time. In high school I dreamed of being a writer, but it felt like something fantastic and unattainable. After all, I was born in 1957, and I was my mother's daughter. I saw what she had grown to believe, and I believed it too: women of my generation were destined to be typists, but for others' words, not our own. We were supposed to become secretaries, not executives.

So I became an escrow officer and typed other people's words. I hated it from the second week but stayed at it for thirteen years. I picked up an occasional glass of wine, which sometimes turned into two or three. At twenty-four I got married, and the accoutrements that come with married life soon followed: the new cars, the furniture, and a brand-new tract home in a dusty, windy San Joaquin County town. After all my years of thinking this would be the answer to all that remained unanswered in my unhappy life, I felt like I was suffocating. In 1986, I left my husband, blindsided, in our new home with the tile roof and ran away to Los Angeles. I didn't think about my life, where I was going, or what I really wanted to do.

Three months after I moved to Los Angeles, my second-oldest sister, Patty, died in an accident. She had been the final connection to the Powers family, if only in looks and temperament. She had our father's looks, his devil-may-care lifestyle. When Dad died and Grandpa disappeared, she was like a woman in exile, wondering where her fellow expatriates had wandered off to, and she eventually battled her own addictions to drugs and alcohol. She drifted from job to job, from man to man. I felt we were a lot alike: birds trapped in a room, fluttering from corner to corner, not seeing the open window. When she died, a vault door slammed shut on the Powers side of the family.

Five years later, I was doing the same work, living the same lifestyle, but the pace had become manic and my unhappiness more desperate. And even though I knew my family history, I drank every day.

In 1995, I decided to go back to school. I also decided that I had to quit drinking. I enrolled in junior college and got a job as an assistant to a real estate agent. I started going to

Alcoholics Anonymous meetings, where I listened and frequently thought of my father and grandfather. Sitting captive in those meetings, I struggled to understand.

I began to write. Then, one day, I pulled *Doc Dillahay* out of the storage trunk and started to read:

> I was worried that September Sunday afternoon. Ma was basting the wild turkey that I'd knocked over for dinner, and every time she opened the cookstove oven I'd get a whiff of the sage dressing and my mouth would water. Then I would think about Monday and what I'd have to face at Tecolote and my tongue would go dry and leathery again. Nervousness would make my stomach squirm.[1]

Doc Dillahay is about John Dillahay, a young man who learns the medical trade in an Arizona town in the 1880s, mentored by the town doctor and town drunk, Dr. Ledinger. There are cattle wars, a brief romance with a pretty girl, redemption with the girl next door, and a shoot-out climax that begins in the town saloon.

All in all, I was rather surprised after reading *Doc Dillahay*. It certainly read well and kept my interest. Of course there were the aggravating modifiers ("he said challengingly"?), but Grandpa's knowledge of frontier medicine was quite impressive, and the story clipped along quite briskly. It definitely didn't follow the standard Western formula I knew from the old movies. With a genre as old-fashioned as the Western, Grandpa dared to write about controversial topics like venereal disease. I would later find out that John Dillahay was modeled after his own father.

Maybe, just maybe, I had underestimated the man.

In 1998 I was a college student at Smith College in Northampton, Massachusetts. I was forty years old and determined to get a bachelor's degree, but I had no idea what I would do with it once I earned it. In my second year I had to decide on a book for an American studies class paper. Sitting in class, I thought of using *Doc Dillahay* as my subject. What a joke, I thought. But the more I thought about it, the more appealing it sounded. At least it wouldn't be a boring paper. After being immersed in Massachusetts academia for over a year, listening to endless pontifications from both students and faculty and drowning in an ocean of political correctness, researching a Western, *his* Western, was the medicine for what ailed me.

Cool. A paper with attitude.

I interviewed my sisters and my mother by phone. I needed to know more about Grandpa. Give me everything you know, I told them. To my frustration, their memories were fragmentary or merely repeated what I already knew. It wasn't a happy picture. According to my mother, Grandpa was irresponsible, a drifter, a periodic drinker.

"You know," she added, "he was a *writer*," emphasizing "writer" as if that explained everything. Her specific memories of her former father-in-law were fragmentary and mysterious: when she met my father, the family was living in luxury one day and in a hovel only a few months later.

But my sister Becky recalled a gentle, benevolent man who took her by the hand whenever we visited the bookstore. She could take home a book, any book, he told her. But inevitably Grandpa would take her by the hand and steer her toward the art section, because he knew she was a budding artist.

But his behavior could be bizarre, she remembered. He would sit up in his bed and announce, "I am going to die in exactly ten seconds. Ten, nine, eight . . ." When he reached "one," he would simply lie down again without another word, his precious books piled around him like subjects of a royal court.

I knew if anyone had answers, it would be my oldest sister, Linda. She had lived with Grandpa and Mary for a brief period during 1966 when she had a job across the bay in San Francisco. When he was sober, he was quiet, serious, and intellectual, she said. As Berkeley exploded outside into a centerpiece of the free-speech movement and Vietnam War protests, Grandpa sat for hours in his apartment and listened to talk radio. But when he drank, he mutated into a venomous bomb that exploded without warning. He drifted into suicidal behavior, scaring the hell out of his wife and granddaughter.

"I'm going to jump out of the window!" he'd yell, sprinting across the room only to stop at the windowsill, just before he would have had to make good on his threat.

One day, Linda came home and Grandpa was perched next to his radio next to the window. It was the time of the sexual revolution in Berkeley, and the radio talk shows were full of it.

"What do you think of this free love business?" Grandpa asked Linda as she opened up a can of soup. She replied in some general, noncommittal manner, trying to keep things peaceful.

"Well," he finished, "when you're done with your chores, you can jump into bed with me."

He might have been kidding. But he might have been serious. More than likely he was drunk. Linda, in retrospect, admits that as a nineteen-year-old with limited exposure to the adult world, and especially men, she might have overreacted. In any event, it took her only a few seconds to leave the house and flee to Mom and the rest of us in the safety of Livermore.

Mom called Mary and told her. She refused to let us see Grandpa again. Linda went back to get her clothes. When she entered the apartment, Grandpa was sitting on the bed, quite upset. She had taken it the wrong way, he said.

As Linda told me this story, I stopped taking notes, trying

to digest the significance of what she was telling me. Was this why we never saw Grandpa again?

As I finished my paper on *Doc Dillahay*, I couldn't stop thinking of Grandpa sitting on that bed, alone, after Linda left.

I turned the paper in on a cold day in December, the Smith campus darkening under winter clouds. But I knew I wasn't finished. I felt cheated somehow, disbelieving that so little could remain from a person's life. Grandpa still felt distant and unreal to me, and still something of a jerk.

Back in my room, I looked at *Doc Dillahay*'s dust jacket again. I read every word. It was as if I'd gained my eyesight after being blind for forty years.

"Born in 1905 in Little River, Kansas . . ."

"All in all Mr. Powers has published, he figures, some 10,000,000 words of fiction."

Ten million words? He must have been drunk when he told them that one, I thought.

"A good bit of it appeared in Street and Smith's old *Wild West Weekly*, where he originated such two-gun characters as 'Kid Wolf,' 'Sonny Tabor,' and 'Johnny Forty-Five'—'all under pen names, thank heavens,' he adds."

I thought of his pen name, Ward Stevens, from the little book *Spook Riders on the Overland*.

"Have you tried to research his pen name?" my friend Lisa Johnson had asked me once when I'd complained about the lack of information. No, I'd answered, confident that it would be a waste of time. The only book he'd written under the name Ward Stevens was that Big Little Book, and that wasn't a *real* book–more like something you'd find in a toy store. It would never show up on an Internet search.

I threw on my coat and headed down the hill to the school library.

The early afternoon light filtered in through the venetian blinds in the computer room. The semester was over, so the room was deserted except for a lone man, probably a gradu-ate student from another college, sitting three chairs down. Tall cabinets holding the old card catalog hovered behind my chair, like mute sentinels observing every word I typed into the computer.

I typed in "Stevens, Ward."

Up popped a book title and the description "A New Little Big Book."

Spook Riders on the Overland, a Freckles Malone story. The book I had seen when I was a child.

In shock, I scrolled down.

Wanted—Sonny Tabor: A Western Story. Copyright: 1931. Chelsea House.

Buckskin and Bullets: A Western Story.

Kid Wolf: A Western Story.

Little Big Books, I found out, were children's books popu-lar during the Great Depression. The originating series was called Big Little Books and was started in 1932 by the Whit-man Publishing Company. These were of the same physical format as *Spook Riders on the Overland*: usually three and a half by four and a half inches, and because there was a black-and-white illustration opposite each page of text, they were quite thick at about four hundred pages. Most featured radio pro-gram and movie characters, comic book heroes—Dick Tracy, Tom Mix, Buck Jones, Flash Gordon, Little Orphan Annie, Mickey Mouse—and most of them were written in-house by authors hired by the publisher. Other books were reprints of pulp stories. Eventually other companies put out their own version of the Big Little Book. *Spook Riders on the Overland, Buckskin and Bullets,* and *Johnny Forty-five* were published by the Saalfield Company, who coined theirs "Little Big Books." As for Chelsea House, which published *Wanted—Sonny Tabor* and *Kid Wolf,* I assumed it was a similar publisher.

Grandpa's Little Big Books were locked up tight in unlikely

places like Bowling Green University and Wellesley College, thousands of miles from the dusty drugstore stands in my imagination. I tried to check them out via the Smith interlibrary service, but these little tomes were too fragile to be checked out and were kept in their respective libraries' special collections, next to volumes of Shakespeare and rare first editions. But there was one exception: *Wanted—Sonny Tabor*. There was one copy in a library in Flagstaff, Arizona. When it arrived at Smith, I hurriedly walked down to the library to pick it up.

The student behind the circulation desk placed a gray book on the counter. But it looked like a regular book, of normal size and proportion. This wasn't a Little Big Book. There was no clumsy watercolor of cowboys adorning the cover, only the title: *Wanted—Sonny Tabor* in bright red. This can't be Grandpa's, I thought. He didn't write any regular novels other than *Doc Dillahay*. What if Ward Stevens was someone else?

"Wait a minute," I said to the student, who was about to scan the book. "This might not be what I'm looking for." I opened the book to the middle: "'We shore will. But doggone me if yuh don't seem might cocksure about givin' me the slip.' The sheriff grinned at Sonny."[2]

I shut the book. Definitely Grandpa's.

———

Every one of the six, with the exception of young Moffitt, had heard much of "Sonny" Tabor—one of the most-feared desperadoes of the Southwest. The very name was enough to chill the hearts of those who had heard of his deeds. "Sonny" sounded mild enough, but no one along the border was so fast and sure with a six-shooter, or so fearless in fight. He was the thorn in the sides of all law officers from Yuma to El Paso.[3]

Sonny is a "young hombre," perpetually nineteen with a youthful face and frank blue eyes, who was wrongfully accused of cold-blooded murder and has been on the lam ever since. Despite being a fugitive, he manages to fight for what's right and turn in all those in black hats who dare to cross his path. It helps that he is the swiftest, most accurate gunman in the West and has Houdini-like talents when it comes to escaping the law—usually just before he gets to the gallows—or surviving multiple gunshot wounds.

There's plenty about Sonny to tell the reader that he is not what the law thinks he is. He has what appears to be a dimple in his cheek, which is really a bullet scar. The dimple and his easy smile and boyish looks tell the reader he's an all-around guy. He's not tall or imposing, but small and catlike. He wears a blue-and-white checked shirt, a cream-colored Stetson, and well-worn brown chapajaros and two Colt .45s with smooth pearl handles that hang low on his thighs. His clothes are dusty and threadbare from his years as a fugitive.

In the first chapter of *Wanted—Sonny Tabor*, a posse of men headed by rancher Ed Stewart ambushes Sonny and shoots enough lead into him to kill ten men. Stewart is stunned to find the outlaw still breathing. He hauls Sonny up onto a horse and takes the boy back to his ranch to recuperate before turning him over to the sheriff. Stewart's wife, Ma, who instinctively knows that Sonny is innocent, tends to Sonny's wounds. As Sonny heals he learns to trust Ma, and eventually he tells her how he became a outlaw.

"I killed a man," Sonny confessed, in a hushed voice. "I shot a man when I was a kid—about fourteen years old. It was this way, Ma: I didn't have any folks, any mother, like you, or maybe it wouldn't have happened. I had to shine boots for a living—had to drift from saloon to saloon. Well, one day a man tried to make me take a drink."

"And what did you do?" Ma demanded, with interest.

"He had a quirt and began beating me with it when I wouldn't do as he said. A man I knew tried to help me, and this drunken fellow drew a knife on him and would've killed him, if I hadn't run behind the bar and picked up a gun that was there. I shot him."

"And then?"

"Well, since then I've been on the run, a hunted man."[4]

Sonny remains a fugitive, shooting only in self-defense or at those who are wicked at heart and threaten the innocent. But to the outside world, his murders are always viewed as cold-blooded and only add fuel to his already infamous legend. By the time of his capture he has killed ten men and is accused of killing an eleventh, and eventually a reward of sixty-five hundred dollars is offered for Sonny, dead or alive.

I walked down to school one Saturday in February. Although snow still cradled the woods around the campus, it was starting to look tired and stale. A perfect day to plan my spring break, a trip to the Florida Keys, by researching the Internet. While I'm at it, I thought, I'll see if there's anything about Little River.

As soon as I typed in the name "Little River" the Web site for the town appeared, complete with photographs of the water tower and a bright city park bordered by flowers. Little River is located in Rice County near the Little Arkansas River, it says. Population: 496. "This is a town with a lot of civic pride. Downtown is clean and neat with new sidewalks and well-painted buildings."[5] It certainly looks like a pleasant town. There are Web sites for the churches, schools, library, businesses, and government. I e-mailed the town library and asked if the town had a historical society. I'm looking for information on Paul Powers, son of Dr. John H. Powers, I wrote. I received a reply almost immediately: yes, there was the Young Historical Society, staffed by Lillie Whiteman.

I called Lillie. A pleasant woman, she didn't remember my grandfather, but she certainly remembered my great-grandfather. In fact, she said, he had delivered Lillie's mother into the world.

I received her package after a week or so, and I was surprised by how much information there was. There were articles in a local newspaper that highlighted the history of Little River, one of the articles accompanied by a photograph of Dr. John H. Powers. The article discussed Dr. Powers's first medical practice and his later position as manager of the town hospital. The photograph was of a tall, lean, dark-haired man sitting in his first medical office in Mitchell, Kansas, in 1902. It was a small office and sparsely furnished: obviously a new doctor's office. Forceps hang on the wall above a shelf of medical bottles and a few medical books.

Dr. Powers was quite handsome. He had an angular face, not the softer face with full cheeks of my grandfather. He didn't look like my grandfather at all.

A few days later I received another envelope from Lillie. She had transcribed bits of information from different newspaper articles and consolidated them onto one piece of paper. The first was a thunderbolt: "June 24, 1920: Paul Powers, son of Dr. Powers, accidentally shot himself in the chest Friday morning. He seems to be doing nicely."[6]

A few weeks after the Sonny Tabor book arrived, I trooped down to the library at Smith to meet with a research librarian. I wasn't looking forward to it. The first time I met with Pam she had been very pleasant and helpful, but the results hadn't been encouraging. We spent what seemed like hours pouring through dusty journals and indexes, looking up Ward Stevens and Paul Powers, only to come up with the same titles. *Wanted—Sonny Tabor. Kid Wolf: A Western Story.* Nothing new. As for the magazines, she had advised me that it shouldn't be too hard to find them. There were archives that hold countless numbers of long-expired periodicals. But finding your grandfather's stories—well, I'd have to go through each magazine by hand.

I pictured hundreds of hours spent in stuffy libraries, thousands of dollars spent . . .

Pam had a strange look on her face when I walked up to the desk. It was as if she had been waiting for me.

She had gone ahead and decided to research the name "Sonny Tabor" on the Internet.

Yes, I've done this already, I thought, impatient. Nothing had come up except the book. Hadn't we done this a dozen times already?

But this time, she said, she had asked for results for any "series" under that name.

She handed me a sheet of paper.

It read: "held at Syracuse University: Sonny Tabor radio series. Eighteen radio scripts. 1940–1949."

A radio series? That was the last thing I expected to find. No one in my family had ever mentioned one. It didn't sound like something that was highly successful, but it certainly wouldn't have happened if the Sonny Tabor book had been a failure.

And what did Syracuse University have to do with it?

I returned to the computer and started another search under Street & Smith and Syracuse.

The university, I quickly found out, held the archives for Street & Smith, which was, I learned from the Syracuse Web site, a true "fiction factory." They published pulp fiction magazines and dime novels from 1864 to the mid-twentieth century, launching thirty-six weekly publications, thirty-nine paperback libraries, sixty magazines, thirteen comic books, six clothbound libraries, three handbooks, and seventeen yearbooks and annuals. From the first, *Ainslee's* in 1898, to the last, *Living for Young Homemakers* in 1947, the company launched 174 different titles.

The weekly publications, most of which were launched in the nineteenth century, were the predecessors of the company's huge stable of pulp fiction magazines. Many of Street & Smith's magazines were closely identified with the pulp fiction era: *Top-Notch* in 1910, *Detective Story Magazine* in 1915, *Western Story Magazine* in 1919, *Love Story Magazine* in 1921, *Wild West Weekly* in 1927, *The Shadow* in 1931, *Astounding Stories* in 1933, *Doc Savage* in 1933, the *Avenger* in 1939, and on and on. There were also clothbound series and comics. Street & Smith's subsidiaries, such as Chelsea House, published reprinted stories in novel form, such as *Wanted—Sonny Tabor*, which is a compilation of five Sonny Tabor stories.

I called the library's Special Collections Department. The woman who answered the phone said yes, *Wild West Weekly* was part of the collection. Records of the authors were incomplete, she said, but they could send me copies of receipts showing when Grandpa had been paid for his work. I thanked her and hung up, expecting a few slips of papers listing maybe half a dozen stories. Still, this was incredibly exciting.

When the package arrived it seemed rather thick for what I was expecting. I opened the envelope and pulled out copies of "Manuscript Tracers," which were bookkeeping receipts the size of five- by seven-inch index cards. Dated from 1937 to 1943, they listed the author's name and address, how many words each story consisted of, the title of the story, and the amount paid to the author. The author on each one: Paul Powers.

I sifted through the copies, looking at the addresses: San Diego, El Cajon, Laguna Beach, Santa Fe, Orange, Santa Ana.

The titles were quaint, some hilarious: "Gun Thunder on

Agony Trail." "A Tomb for the Kid Wolf Hombre." "Where Sheriffs Fear to Tread," and my favorite: "The Devil Rides a Pinto."

I counted the receipts.

There were more than eighty stories.

I couldn't deny it anymore: my grandfather had been a pulp fiction writer. This was what Mom was talking about when she mentioned that he had written for the "Western magazines." It seemed like such a dubious distinction. Perhaps he had just dabbled in them, I hoped. A hobby. Something he did just to pay the bills.

Nevertheless, I started to read whatever I could find on the history of pulp fiction.

I had always associated the term "pulp fiction" with images of lurid magazine covers with detectives in fedoras, dark corners, plenty of blood and guns. Skulls. Women in bondage. "The Shadow" is the only pulp fiction character that I have ever heard of.

In reality, pulp fiction was a publishing phenomenon that created thousands of characters and involved hundreds of different magazine titles during the first half of the twentieth century. Pulp fiction wasn't only gangsters and detectives, it was jungle, desert, and sea adventures; Canadian Mounties stories; Civil War, World War I, and spy stories; police, courtroom, and prison stories; ghost, supernatural, and weird tales; frontier and science fiction; and of course Westerns.

Pulp fiction magazines, along with their predecessors—dime novels and cheap fiction magazines of the nineteenth century—were one of the most popular forms of entertainment from the Civil War to World War II. But they were most popular during one of the bleakest times in American history. During the Great Depression, as many as 250 different varieties of glossy, colorful covers almost jumped out of newsstands every week, promising unimaginable drama, suspense, and romance. The stories always had a happy ending and justice was always served, which was quite comforting in the real world, which had become illogical, cold, and cruel. Reading a pulp magazine provided a few hours of diversion and comfort in a very uncertain world.

For a dime or fifteen cents, readers could buy a magazine of two to three short novels, three or four shorter stories, an editorial column or two, a list of pen pals for those hungering to hear from someone from another, better part of the world, and several pages of advertisements promising everything from a happy marriage to a fulfilling career to rupture relief. They were seven- by ten-inch magazines of 128 to 144 pages, depending on the publisher and how lush or lean the times were. The paper was cheap, rough pulp paper, the binders were flimsy, and the borders were irregularly cut. Except for their lurid covers, there were no pictures, save for a few black-and-white illustrations at the beginning of each story.

Of the scores of themes offered in pulps, the Western was one of the most popular. Between 1920 and 1945, at least 162 different Western magazines hit the newsstands at one point or another, resulting in the depression era being called the Western's golden age.[7] At one point in 1940 there were thirty-six different pulp Western magazines on newsstands, just waiting to be bought and read.[8]

It made sense. The depression, after all, brought poverty, hunger, and desperation to America in epic proportions. Not surprisingly, many wished to escape, yet there was no way to physically leave their grinding hunger and worry, because it was everywhere. There were no unemployment benefits, no Social Security, no welfare assistance. There were a few charitable organizations, but their assistance was spread thin and was completely overwhelmed by the enormous numbers of hungry people that waited in line. Hunger was so widespread that people resorted to eating weeds and fighting over city garbage cans for food. Banks failed in epidemic proportions, customers' deposits evaporating overnight. In 1931 alone, banks failed at the rate of thirty-eight a week.

But the Western promised escape from it all. In the pulp Western there is no ambiguity: the good guy always wins, and the landscape always soars. Pulp heroes have impeccable manners and show righteous outrage when the occasion calls for it. And the occasions are frequent. Their eyes glimmer with hate over the injustice of the downtrodden, and they calmly mow down their enemies with dead-eye aim.

With a pulp magazine in their hands, readers could, at least for a few hours, live on the big ranch rather than in the stifling apartment in the city. They could escape to where they could breathe the air, be in control of their own destiny, and derive a certain satisfaction from story lines that meted out appropriate judgment to characters based on their actions. Westerns allowed readers to pretend, at least temporarily, that their problems could be solved with a gunfight on main street or with a sheriff's swing of a saloon door.

Pulp fiction magazines were descendants of several different types of reading material that had evolved over the nineteenth century. Cheap weeklies, many of them inspired by the "penny dreadfuls" produced in England, featured wildly implausible adventure themes during the early 1800s, long before mass production was even thought of. Dime novels—magazines packed with heroes spouting flowery language and rescuing maidens from seedy characters in locales ranging from the Wild West frontier to raging seas to the deep Amazon jungle—were immensely popular even before the Civil War. Weeklies and dime novels had two common denominators: a tough, individualistic, adventurous hero and a thrilling plot.

Two brothers with erratic business backgrounds, accompanied by a handsome young upstart, were the brains behind the most successful publication phenomenon of the nineteenth century, the dime novel. Before setting up their own company in 1850, Irwin and Erastus Beadle had wandered through apprenticeships in which they learned typesetting, bookbinding, and stereotyping. Erastus was a born entrepreneur, always looking for new ventures even when the existing ones were failing. But other than publishing two genteel periodicals, the brothers seemed to spend most of the their time moving offices, forming and dissolving partnerships, and surviving management crises. Erastus even pulled up stakes in 1857 and left for Nebraska to make a fortune in real estate. He showed up six months later at Irwin's doors, disheveled and broke. Robert Adams, a young man who probably had more patience than sense, put up with the brothers' constant business "adjustments" and handled the nuts and bolts of publishing their magazines and occasional books.[9]

After several management and partnership changes, all three moved to New York. Knowing that songbooks were very popular, Irwin published a *Dime Song Book*, charging ten cents. For once, a Beadle brother had an unqualified success. He then published "dime books" on various topics, including "Every Man His Own Gardner," "Republican Campaign Songster" and "Budget of Fun." When the company started to see more black ink than red, Irwin decided to branch out. Seeing that the market for fiction seemed to be infinite, Irwin began a series of what he called "dime novels," each running around thirty thousand words. The first dime novel, *Malaeska: The Indian Wife of the White Hunter*, by Mrs. Ann S. Stephens, an established popular writer, was actually a reprint from the *Ladies Companion*. Irwin paid Stephens $250 for the privilege, an investment that would eventually pay off a hundredfold. Within five years he had sold five million copies of various dime novel series. One story alone, *Seth Jones; Or, the Captives of the Frontier*, written by Edward Ellis and published in 1860, eventually sold 400,000 copies.

The Civil War was a boon to Erastus Beadle, ever the opportunist. He focused on supplying the soldiers with dime novels to read during idle time, a brilliant move that introduced a new audience to stories that promised breathtaking adventure week after week, and resulted in his selling four million dime novels.

It wasn't long before Beadle and Adams saw competition from other companies.

Street & Smith had begun modestly in 1855 with the partnership of Francis Scott Street and Francis Shubael Smith. Street, a mere twenty-four years old, was in the business department of the *New York Sunday Dispatch*, a periodical known for sensational fiction, most of it written by the thirty-six-year-old Smith. It was the perfect marriage of business and creativity. They began their publishing career by purchasing the *Dispatch* in 1855, renaming it the *New York Weekly Dispatch*. At first sales were lukewarm, but they stuck to it, and it didn't hurt that they managed to hang on during the panic of 1857, when many publications folded. Smith continued to write, but eventually he began to recruit other writers. A man of "strong moral convictions," he wanted to start a publication for boys. It would be several years before that dream would be realized. But his high ethical standards didn't prevent him from making shrewd business choices. For example, he hired a popular writer, Charlotte Brame, changed her name to Bertha Clay, and proclaimed her to be a "discovery" of Street & Smith's.[10]

The company advertised the *New York Weekly* on billboards— a fairly new medium—along the Pennsylvania Railroad between Philadelphia and New York City. The billboards were such a successful publicity tool that the firm plastered posters across New York City advertising the *Weekly*. They also began to distribute first installments of serials to thousands of news dealers across the country and to potential customers free of charge. The cliffhanger ending almost guaranteed a sale of the remainder of the series.

For all his business acumen, Street began to lose interest in the *Weekly* and became more involved with his real estate investments. When Street died in 1883, Smith's youngest son, Ormond, bought Street's interest in the company from his estate. For the next fifty-five years, the Smith family maintained total control over the company, Ormond ruling with an iron hand for fifty of them. When Francis Smith died in 1887, his son George took over as vice president under Ormond's presidency, but it was Ormond who instilled fear in the hearts of most of his employees.

By the time their father died, the Smith brothers had already launched their first hit with the Nick Carter series in 1886. The company launched into paperback books called "libraries," which were collections of stories, most of them virtually indistinguishable from each other. By the 1890s they had successfully launched such series as *Tip Top Weekly*, the Frank Merriwell series, the Yellow Kid series, the Diamond Dick Library, and their most successful dime novel series, the Buffalo Bill series.

In the early 1890s, another publisher, Frank Munsey, was trying to find ways to keep his magazine, the *Argosy*, afloat. He knew that many of his readers, most of whom belonged to the working class, loved to read short fiction.[11] But many of his readers could not afford the more expensive magazines such as *Harper's* and *Scribner's*. They probably didn't care for them anyway; these more "cultured" magazines packed their issues with advertisements, and the fiction was sparse and staid.

Munsey decided to use cheap wood pulp paper, the type used for many newspapers. Pulp paper was cheaper because it was void of the treatment used for more expensive magazine and book paper. Not treating the paper made it highly acidic and eventually extremely fragile, a trait that would be the bane of pulp fiction readers and, later, historians and archivists.

Munsey omitted all illustrations except those on the cover, thinking that readers cared more for the stories themselves, and slashed the price to ten cents. He found that he could print a good deal of fiction in one issue. The *Argosy* debuted in 1896, encapsulated in a cover quite plain in contrast to the pulps that would follow. The returns for the *Argosy* were surprisingly good—enough to keep Munsey, who ruthlessly dropped magazines the minute there was any hint of profit loss, from killing it.[12] The *Argosy* survived in its new format and flourished to the point that soon it was selling a half million copies a month.

Dime novels were saturated with western heroes, such as mountain men and "Indian hunters." Then, in 1902, Owen Wister's *The Virginian* was published. The book's basic elements—a lone, chivalrous cowboy who rights wrongs, a romance, and a final gunfight—became the standard for the formula Western for the next century. The cowboy quickly became the staple of the dime novel.

That same year, Frank Tousey, who had been publishing dime novels for several years, created a magazine about a young mutant of Buffalo Bill called Young Wild West, and called it *Wild West Weekly*. Young Wild West, nicknamed "Wild," was a handsome blond dressed in buckskins who traveled the countryside on his magnificent sorrel stallion, a "perfect picture of a dashing young Westerner."[13] Wild was an adventurer who owned mine stock in the Black Hills and thus could afford to roam the countryside in pursuit of adventure. His exploits were narrated in thirty-thousand-word novels every week by a storyteller known only as "An Old Scout."

By 1930 the Street & Smith building at 79 Seventh Avenue, New York, seven stories high, was a beacon of success in a city staggering under the weight of the depression. The building vibrated from top to bottom from the presses on the second floor that had run nonstop, day and night, for more than twenty years. When the building was erected in 1907, the company grandiosely proclaimed it "the greatest publishing house in the world."[14]

It was, if not the greatest, surely the most prolific, and certainly one of the busiest. The building reeked of ink. The warehouse stored enormous rolls of pulp paper, each half as big as a grown man. An early proponent of forest clearing, the company unabashedly claimed that if the gargantuan rolls of paper were unwound and placed end to end, the paper would reach from New York City to Cleveland. Stacks of returned magazines crowded the hallways. Warehouse rooms that covered almost entire floors were packed full of shelving for the magazines it published. From the executive offices, with their paneled walls, thick carpeting, and rolltop desks, to the bullpens in which half a dozen artists were crammed, the company was the true fiction factory. Street & Smith was king of the pulp fiction world.

Every move the company made was under the eye of Ormond Smith. Control was all-important. Everything they published, from the dime novels, the weeklies, the pulp fiction, to the 1955 book celebrating their hundred-year anniversary, *The Fiction Factory*, was carefully supervised and was required to follow the chief's exacting requirements. According to the book, everything the company published was an "unqualified success." Ormond Smith is portrayed as distant and remote but with a heart of gold. The company's magazine heroes were the greatest fictional heroes of all time. Just like its subject, *The Fiction Factory* is confident, calculating, and careful.

Close reading, however, reveals some hints of how the company really ran. "The only commodity cheaper than paper was editorial talent."[15] Editors and writers were considered both expendable and rarely worth more than the pittance the industry was paying. But no expense was spared for printing equipment, engraving machines, and folding machines. Although staff were poorly paid, they were expected to dress rich. One day Ormond Smith spotted an engraver without a coat or tie. "See how essential that man is. If we can spare him, get rid of him." Knowing the engraver's value to the company, Ormond's brother convinced him to keep the man.[16]

Frank Tousey's company wasn't doing as well. By 1920, circulation for the *Wild West Weekly* had plummeted. Young Wild West was getting a little long in the tooth and was no longer a novelty. By the early 1920s the series had deteriorated to the point where new issues were just reproductions of earlier ones.

Ormond Smith bought *Wild West Weekly* in 1927. Street & Smith had plans: Young Wild West would still be the dominant character, but his name would be changed to Billy West. Circle J in Montana was his outfit, and he was joined by three sidekicks: Buck Foster, Joe Scott, and a Chinese cook named Sing Lo. But new heroes would be added to the new *Wild West Weekly*; the plan was to attract a young and exuberant audience. Ronald Oliphant, for a while an associate editor of *Detective Story Magazine* and later the editor of *Thrill Book*, was put in charge of the magazine and ordered to start looking for new writers.

Even though it was the end of February, there was very little snow in Northampton. The winter had been a mild one, and the clouds that glided in uniform promised that winter was all but over. Students in the computer center, however, looked glum and tense: this was the darkest time of the semester, when no end was in sight. I sat down at a computer and typed "Kansas" into the search engine.

I kept my coat on as I flipped back and forth between Web sites, losing track of where I was in cyberspace but not really caring. I was restless, not really sure what I was looking for and not caring. Kansas historical societies kept popping up. Researching family history seems to be a popular sport in this country. A genealogy bulletin board appeared, where notices were posted requesting information about family history. What the heck, I thought; it's free. I posted a short notice:

Am looking for any information about John Harold Powers I, who was a practicing physician in McPherson until his death in 1931. Am also looking for any information regarding his children, Paul S., Nellie, George, and Phyllis. (Paul is my grandfather. He married Velma Niccum in approximately 1924 in Colorado, and they settled in Little River Kansas in 1925.)

I got up and left and promptly forgot about it. After all, other attempts to find my father's family had been futile. I had occasionally thought about trying to find them, but it always felt like such a huge undertaking, so powerful that I stopped breathing whenever I thought about it. But I doggedly tried again the year before coming to Smith. This was in the days before the Internet, and finding lost families took years, sometimes lifetimes, along with a lot of money and private detectives. I checked out a book on finding lost relatives through government records, eagerly taking it to the library's reading room.

There were plenty of ways to find out, according to this book, using the lost person's Social Security number.

Social Security number? Logically, if I had any information on my grandfather, chances are it would not be his Social Security number. A birth date, maybe. But if I had a person's most valuable identification number, chances are I'd have other information too, making this whole exercise moot. Ridiculous, I thought. I left, utterly discouraged.

I plopped down in the chair the morning after posting the notice. I had a few minutes to check things before my first class.

There was an e-mail from a Steve Somers. E-mail Duane Powers, he told me. He's done quite a bit of research on the Powers family, all the way back to England.

I dutifully followed his instructions. Did he know anything about my grandfather? Was there any chance he knew where my aunt and uncle were?

Mon, 1 Mar 1999

From: Duane Powers
To: Laurie Powers

My father John Roscoe Powers was a first cousin of your grandfather . . . I was born in Little River, Kansas as were most of our cousins . . . In 1933, when I was about 8 years old, we, my mother and dad and grandmother, went to Bisbee, AZ and stayed for a while. My father was looking for work and evidently Paul had suggested that the copper mines there would be opening soon . . . it didn't happen . . . I recall being there and the fact that your grandfather was much better off than we were . . . I have known all my life that he wrote western[s] for the "pulp" magazine . . . .

You didn't mention George Harold Powers and Phyllis Powers who were children of John Harold Powers I second marriage . . . George is a retired MD living in Phoenix, AZ, and Phyllis lives in Columbus, Ohio . . . I'll send you their addresses if you want them.

I gasped. Grandpa's half brother and sister are still *alive?* As if that weren't enough, Duane launched into my grandfather's other children, my aunt and uncle: "George sent to me the following addresses for Tom and Pat, but said that he didn't know if they were still there."

Duane then listed Pat's and Tom's addresses, as casually as if he were writing out a shopping list.

I sent my aunt and uncle duplicate letters shortly after getting Duane's e-mail, hoping that by sending them each one it would double my chances of at least one responding.

March 3, 1999

Dear Mrs. Binkley:

My name is Laurie Powers. I'm writing you this letter because I am looking for an aunt of mine, and your name and address was given to me after I posted a request for information on a Kansas genealogy site on the Internet. I'm wondering if you may be my aunt and, if you are, if we could get reacquainted after many years.

My heart in my throat, I dropped the letters in the mailbox, feeling as if I'd thrown a hand grenade into their living rooms.

March 7, 1999

Dear Laurie:

It was wonderful to hear from you. Yes, I am your Aunt Patricia. I was always sorry that I lost touch with all of you and would be very interested in getting together . . .
    . . . Tom called and told me he had received your letter and wishes you all well. Unfortunately, he is not doing too well these days. Physically, he is fine but his memory is getting very bad—I'm afraid he may have Alzheimer's disease.
    . . . I have boxes of old letters and manuscripts that my folks left that may be of interest to you.

A few days after the school year finished, I rented a car and drove to Syracuse University, hoping to find more information about Grandpa in the Street & Smith archives. I wanted to read some of his stories while I was there. I knew I wouldn't be able to look at all eighty stories, but I'd be able to at least look at a few.

I signed in at the special collections desk and met Carolyn Davis, the librarian. I asked for the *Wild West Weekly* accounting records for the years 1937 through 1943, the years of the receipts that were mailed to me.

Boxes were wheeled out on a cart. Each box contained seven- by ten-inch cards that appeared to be running accounts of stories published through the years. Each card listed eight to ten stories received by various authors. Each story was posted with the day it was received by the publisher, the name of the real author instead of the pseudonym, the title of the story, the date the story was published, how many words the story contained, and what the author was paid.

There were hundreds of cards for each year. The name Paul Powers appeared on roughly half of the cards. Grandpa consistently made more than two hundred dollars per story, at the rate of a penny and a half per word.

Suddenly, I realized that something was missing. *Wanted— Sonny Tabor* had been published in 1931. If Sonny was in book form in 1931, wouldn't he have been in the magazine in 1931 or even earlier? Of the receipts that the curator had mailed to me, what years did they represent? I looked again; they covered 1937 to 1943. What about 1931 to 1937? Why didn't I have any receipts for those years? Suddenly I realized that the researcher whom I had talked to on the phone that day might have pulled only a portion of the receipts.

I asked to see all of the cards from Street & Smith's first issue of *Wild West Weekly*, published in 1927. Nothing the first year. Then, there it was: Grandpa's first story, "The Whispering Gunman," published on October 6, 1928, under his own name. Moving forward, his next story, "Gold in Poverty Canyon," published on November 17, 1928. Then his stories began to appear more frequently. He started to use pen names.

Between October 1928 and March 1929, just a six-month period, my grandfather wrote at least nineteen stories that were printed under no less than eight different pseudonyms as well as his own name. His writing career had been catapulted into the stratosphere almost from the very beginning of the magazine.

By noon I was exhausted and overwhelmed, and I hadn't even looked at the magazines yet. I hadn't even tried to count the number of stories. I found a list that tabulated just Sonny Tabor stories: there were 135. But there were other characters: Kid Wolf, Freckles Malone, Johnny Forty-five, King Kolt, and others. There weren't eighty stories—there were hundreds.

Bleary-eyed, I asked to see the magazines. What years? asked Carolyn. I don't know, I answered. Any year. She rolled out a cart piled with bound volumes. Each volume contained roughly six weeks' worth of issues. I picked one and opened it.

Sonny Tabor and his horse Paint were on the first cover.

Wild West Weekly covers, like those of most pulp magazines, are full of bold reds, yellows, and greens. Cowboys are always punching or shooting, streaks of red flaming out of their pistols like laser beams. The horses are beautiful and usually buckskin, palomino, snow white, pinto, or other unusual colors. They rear and charge like the horses of the Apocalypse, the excitement and fear of the scene reflected in their eyes.

The pages inside are printed on a dull brown paper, brittle with age.

The first few pages are advertisements:

We will make you an Electrical Expert in 90 days
Bright's wines: delicious! Appetizing! Nourishing!
Acid in Your Blood Kills Health and Pep—Kidneys
    Often to Blame
Over 700,000 People have studied music this way

Free—How to Secure a Government Position
Let Kidneys Flush Out 3 lbs. A Day
I Want Men—Tea and Coffee Routes paying up to $60
  a week. No experience necessary. Fords Given.
Hand Out FREE CIGARETTES and earn up to $95 weekly.

Correspondence schools were one of the most frequent buyers of advertisement space. In the February 14, 1931, issue, eleven ads promoting education or better job opportunities appeared: International Correspondence Schools ("If you're a quitter you won't read far in this advertisement"), Coyne Electrical School ("We will make you an electrical expert in 3 months at Coyne"), a division of Coyne called the Radio ("Win Fame and Fortune in Radio!"), the Institute of Applied Science (". . . the great future for YOU as a highly paid Finger Print Expert"), and on and on.

In the early years the magazine featured "Three Complete Western Novelettes" and "Four Complete Western Stories." The word "complete" was important, as many magazines ran serials that continued from week to week, much to the aggravation of readers. Many readers liked *Wild West Weekly* because it promised to keep each story complete. But in the early 1930s the magazine began to run serials, usually consisting of six stories, many of them written by the prolific Walker Tompkins. Readers had mixed feelings about the serials, but the tradition continued into the late 1930s.

The heroes that dominated each issue of the magazine, especially during the early years, accounted for much of *Wild West Weekly*'s popularity. Out of the eight to ten stories in each issue, five to seven would feature heroes like the Circle J partners, Lum Yates, Bud Jones of Texas, the Whistlin' Kid, Looshis Carey, the Ranny Kid, and the Bar U Twins.

Some of the longest-running characters were the Circle J partners. Billy West, Joe Scott, Buck Foster, and Sing Lo were all descendants of the early *Wild West Weekly* that began in

1902. Billy is a boyish, handsome fellow with kindly gray eyes who rides a chestnut stallion named Danger. Although Billy is in charge of the Montana Circle J Ranch and is certainly the most level-headed of the group, many of the stories focus in the antics of Buck and Joe, who manage to get into trouble or fall into incidents where their help is needed in catching a villain. Buck is a grizzled "veteran" with a large, drooping moustache and a propensity for saying "Wal, I'll be a horned toad!" Joe, on the other hand, is a hot-tempered redhead and an expert tracker. The two continually bicker but are always there for each other. The Circle J stories were written by several different men using the pseudonym Cleve Endicott over the years. During the first few years Norman Hay wrote the stories, and then Ronald Oliphant wrote one a month. Later, Houston Irvine and Hal Davenport would write Circle J stories.

The Whistlin' Kid, created by J. Allan Dunn under the pseudonym Emery Jackson, was another early popular hero. A range detective for the Cattlemen's Association, the Whistlin' Kid whistled only one song: "The Cowboy's Lament." The Silver Kid, created by T. W. Ford, was a hero who was normal other than his penchant for wearing silver and having his horse's saddle decked out in silver. Some short stories featured regular heroes like the Bar U Twins, Tom and Jerry Carter. Many heroes were Texas Rangers, like Bud Jones of Company F and Hungry and Rusty. One of the early favorites, showing up almost every week, was Lum Yates, a cowpuncher from Missouri. He is a simple guy with no superhero characteristics, with a gangly partner named Zeke of unknown origin. But the feature that endeared him to many readers is his small, scrawny yellow dog named Job, who fits into a feedbag that dangles from Lum's saddle horn. Job is Lum's sensor, growling at threatening men before Lum has a clue that he could be in danger.

Some of these, like Sonny Tabor, Kid Wolf, the Silver Kid,

and the Circle J "pards," appeared for the duration of the magazine's fifteen years. Others, like Dapper Donnelly and Blackston Bangs, appeared for perhaps a dozen stories before disappearing. Sonny Tabor and Kid Wolf appeared every third or fourth week—Sonny the first week, Kid Wolf the next, a week or two where other writers' heroes appear, and so forth.

Kid Wolf was an independently wealthy rancher from the Rio Lobo, who wore a fringed buckskin outfit, spoke with a heavy Texas drawl, and rode a magnificent snow-white steed named Blizzard. In his first story, "The Gunman of Monterey," Kid Wolf arrives in the sunny town of Monterey, California, during a festival. He is a mysterious man to the natives, but it isn't long before he establishes his reputation. A hired vigilante of sorts, he has come to Monterey at the request of Don Diego, governor and chief villain of the province, but the Kid is unaware of why he has been summoned. When he meets Don Diego, he learns that the governor wishes to take over the ranch of a white man, O'Hara. Kid, of course, refuses: "Kid Wolf got to his feet. 'Yes,' he said softly, 'I am just a soldier of fortune—a gunman. But listen! I have always fought fo' the under dawg. I've always fought fo' the weak against the strong, and I've always tried to fight fo' the side that is in the right. Yo' want me to help yo' in yo' underhand dealings, Mistah Gov'nor? Yo' want my answer?'"[17]

Kid leaves in disgust and takes off for the O'Hara ranch to warn them of Don Diego's intentions. After several plot turns, including being ambushed, captured, returned to Don Diego, sentenced to death, and then escaping from prison, Kid eventually finds his way to the O'Hara ranch. There he has a chance to show off some of his gun talent to O'Hara's son and Craig, the foreman: "Kid Wolf got up, stretched lazily and picked up two of the flowerpots. He held them both out at arm's length, shoulder-high. Then he dropped them. His two guns roared, and both pots flew to bits before they had dropped to the level of his waist."[18]

Kid is handy with a gun, but his trademark is a Bowie knife hidden in a sheath between his shoulder blades. He rarely uses it, since he prefers to use his well-worn revolvers, but when he does, he flings the knife with deadly accuracy. It always ends up lodged in the throat of the aggressors.

Grandpa created another hero, Johnny Forty-five, using the pen name Andrew Griffin, which he shared with other *Wild West Weekly* writers. Johnny Forty-five didn't get as much air time as Sonny and Kid, but he was one of the magazine's most memorable heroes. "The Fightin' Poet" first appeared in the July 20, 1929, issue. Poet Pete is an enigma who shows up at the Oriental Saloon wearing bright purple angora chaps, patent leather boots, and brand-new cowboy hat, shirt, and vest. He keeps his mouth shut, even though he's goaded by curious cowboys who want to know who this bizarre stranger is. When he finally opens his mouth, it is in the form of four-line verses, but ever mindful that young boys will be reading his story in Prohibition times:

> Whisky makes me very ill,
>   Beer gives me quite a pain;
> So kindly fill a water glass,
>   And I will be refreshed again![19]

In later stories, Poet Pete eventually mutates into Johnny Socrates, otherwise known as Johnny Forty-five, who is continually thrown into hot water by his bumbling sidekick, Deputy U.S. Marshal George Krumm. Johnny Forty-five also has a peculiar habit of rolling cigarettes but not smoking them. His explains in this four-line wonder that it keeps his fingers nimble for shooting purposes:

I promised ma I wouldn't smoke
Till I was sixty-one
But rollin' cigs is mighty fine
For fingers that trigger a gun.[20]

Another one of Grandpa's characters was Freckles Malone. Freckles seems to be the most "normal" of all of Grandpa's heroes, namely, he isn't a wrongly accused killer, a buckskin-wearing Texan, or a purple-chap-wearing poet. Freckles is merely a Pony Express rider who is good with a gun. He does, however, have a sidekick, Swen Svenson, a blond and gangly Swedish cook for the riders on the Overland Trail, whose Herculean size and strength are a throwback to Paul Bunyan. Indeed, Svenson is simple-minded and devoted to Freckles; his mission in life is to feed Freckles his favorite meal of flapjacks with a side dish of fried venison. Svenson's dialect ("Freckles he ban late! . . . Dat not happen very often, by Yiminy!") underscores the fellow's simplicity. But Svenson can be counted on in a pinch, turning into a "angry bull," swatting down adversaries with his enormous hands "like a woodchopper."[21]

Some heroes were "good" outlaws like Sonny Tabor. The Oklahoma Kid, a Walker Tompkins character, had to shoot a bullying, crooked rancher in his hometown. Unfortunately, the bully had been a rich man with many connections who forced the Kid to go on the run. Now the Kid chases men accused of the same crimes he has been wrongly accused of. His archenemy is "lank, bug-eyed, rattle-headed Deputy Ed Sparks," who, in "The Oklahoma Kid's Rancho Visit," catches the kid by surprise: "'Sky them paws, Ugly!' the deputy whooped. 'I've got yuh at last, yuh ornery little snake. Hands up, or I yank these triggers!'"[22]

But even though these heroes use their guns when the need arises, they are not guns for hire. When gang leader Harris tries to hire Kid Wolf for mercenary work in "Turkeys and Buzzards for Kid Wolf," the Kid sets him straight:

Under the bronze of his lean face Kid Wolf had gone pale with anger.

"I'm not to be hiahed fo' murdah!" his voice crackled like an electric spark.

"Murder?" Harris shrugged. "What are yuh talkin' about? Who said anything about murder? I understand that my men are callin' themselves the Death Buzzards," he went on with a humorous chuckle, "but thet's a joke. Only to throw a scare—"

A joke! The Texan's hot Southern temper flamed suddenly beyond control. Had it not been for John Harris's white hairs, his sixty years, the Kid would probably have closed his fist—or filled it! As it was, he reached across the desk and gave Harris an open-handed slap in the face that made a report like a pistol shot.[23]

It helped if the hero could be faced with real-life dilemmas that the depression reader could relate to. Sonny Tabor's clothes are shabby, and he continually wanders the countryside of Arizona and New Mexico looking for employment: "Sonny was looking for a job; he always worked when a job was to be had, which wasn't often, for the law quickly found him out. In spite of the fact that he was a 'wanted' man, he worked whenever possible at the only game he knew—punching cows."[24] Despite knowing that the entire Southwest is after his head, Sonny tries to get hired on small, isolated cattle ranches in Arizona or New Mexico. Like the worker of the 1930s, he was just an honest guy looking for an honest day's work.

While the standard pulp hero depicts all the things that were wanting in the world, villains have cruel and calculating eyes, disfigured faces, crooked and disingenuous smiles, and repulsive smells. They usually have dark complexions, and many are of Mexican descent. They are the gangs that wait in ambush in the desert at night, the hired assassins employed by the greedy ranchers to torture and kill homesteaders who are unlucky enough to own rich cattle land, the sadistic accomplices who brand a young rancher's forehead as a means of extracting information, and the band of desperadoes who stake a white man to the ground, face up and spread eagle, cut off his eyelids, and leave him for the buzzards. Torture is the calling card of the villain.

American Indians are commonly referred to as "breeds," but in many stories they are allies of the white man. Grey Eagle is a close and valuable assistant to hero Señor Red Mask, a character in stories by Guy Maynard. In "The Devil's Calling Card," hero Colt Drigger is half Cherokee and proud that his mother was the daughter of a Cherokee chief.[25]

Portraits of Asians, almost always Chinese, are so blatantly offensive that they would make any modern reader blanch. Frequently referred to as "chinks," they are subservient but crafty. Sing Lo, the cook who travels with Billy West, Buck, and Joe, is not above lying to get them out of a fix, and he has a weakness for liquor. Sing Lo has a "flat yellow face" and "slant eyes," and has to prove that he is not like "typical" Chinese who apparently are known for their underhandedness. "Me velly honest Chinee!" he blurts to shifty Long Sam Raynor before letting loose of a string of lies.[26] Most of these characteristics were standard fare for many pulp magazines, not just *Wild West Weekly*.

In the early years the stories usually ran along one plot line, namely, the hero chasing one person, with very little variation. In "The Haunted Mustang," a Circle J story in the July 20, 1929, issue, Billy West spends the entire story chasing a mythical wild stallion that has killed one of his own prize horses. In 1930, Circle J stories, usually written by Norman Hay or editor Oliphant, began to change. They moved quickly, with more action and a lot more violence. Stories became more complex, with additional characters complicating the chase, multiple changes of scenes, more conflicts and fistfights, and one or two fatalities in the middle of the story rather than just at the end.

Along those same lines, the use of violence to capture or kill criminals was not as prevalent in the beginning. Criminals were arrested and sent off to be tried and sent to prison rather than killed in confrontations with the hero. Occasionally they were hanged. But over the years, violence became the centrifuge of most stories, including Sonny Tabor and Kid Wolf stories. From the lead sentence on, everything rolls toward a climactic bloody scene. To keep the reader interested, a few shootings in the middle of the story or at least a fistfight was mandatory. Problems can only be solved through shooting and mayhem. Justice had to be meted out in graphic description, yet ironically, never with the use of the words *blood* or *bleed*, as seen in the climaxes of these two Sonny Tabor stories:

Al Bentley, his head smashed like a ripe pumpkin, spun rapidly around on his boot heels and fell without a sound, his unfired Colt still clutched in his hand.

Toke Landus died at almost the same moment. With his heart chopped in two, he took half a dozen running steps, screaming thinly. His gun exploded into the ground as he fell heavily. He rolled over several times and lay still.[27]

The full charge of buckshot hit Mark Seabury in the head, nearly blowing it from his shoulders. It killed the rancher instantly, and dropped him, a bundle of reddened rags, into the snow under the hoofs of his frightened cayuse.[28]

Wild West Weekly always included several columns: "Western Quiz (Quien Sabe?)," a "Fact Story," a pen pal exchange, and "Wrangler's Corner," which published readers' drawings and short stories. "A Chat with the Range Boss" was a colorful version of "Letters to the Editor." In this column, various characters who appeared in the magazine engaged in a running dialogue with each other and the editor, who is thinly disguised as the "Range Boss." Heroes such as Shorty Masters, the Whistlin' Kid, and Buck Foster verbally spar with each other, comment on the mail they have received from readers, answer questions from readers, and select poems from readers for the column, all under the watchful eye of the Range Boss. In the later 1930s it appears that this column dropped the characters' interaction and was used by the editor to discuss various interesting anecdotes, many times writing about authors and the background of some of their stories. Writers were invited to write in, but if they wrote under a pen name, the pseudonym signed the letter.

One hundred and ninety seven writers dipped their pens into the *Wild West Weekly* well at one point or another between 1927 and 1943.[29] The majority came and went after just a few stories, some after only one. Only a fraction were what could be considered the magazine's core. Roughly thirty writers managed to write more than fifty stories each, and of those only fourteen wrote more than a hundred. Both Ronald Oliphant and Francis Stebbins, a later editor, contributed significantly as writers.

Most of the writers used house pseudonyms such as Andrew Griffin, Cleve Endicott, and Nels Anderson. House names were the property of *Wild West Weekly* and were used by the editors at their discretion. For example, the name Nels Anderson was used by thirty-one different writers. Sometimes house names were used in combinations that would dumbfound any bookkeeper trying to keep the books straight. For example, the house name Cleve Endicott was used by other writers writing solo ("by Cleve Endicott"), was used in partnership with other writers using their real names ("by Lee Bond and Cleve Endicott," which could be Lee Bond writing solo or Lee Bond writing with another person), and was used in partnership with other pseudonyms ("by Ward Stevens and Cleve Endicott," which could be one writer, usually Paul Powers, pretending to be two writers and using both pseudonyms, or in rare cases, two writers). Over the fifteen years as a *Wild West Weekly* author, Grandpa used twelve different pseudonyms, although the vast majority were Sonny Tabor and Kid Wolf stories written under the name Ward M. Stevens.

By having a writer publish several stories in one issue under different names, the magazine was using a common marketing tool used by most publishers of pulp fiction. It appeared to the reader that the magazine was providing a diverse collection of stories from different writers, when in fact only three or four writers were responsible for eight to ten stories. As Paul's career with *Wild West Weekly* continued, it was common for him to have two stories in one issue: a novelette under a pen name and a short story under his real name. Sometimes he had as many as three stories in one issue. By the time Sonny Tabor appeared in the summer of 1929, Paul had taken the pen name Ward M. Stevens as his own. He would use that name exclusively for his Sonny Tabor, Kid Wolf, and Freckles Malone stories for the duration of the magazine. He also used almost every house name on the books, including Andrew Griffin, Philip F. Deere, and Dean McKinley.[30]

Many writers had lives as colorful as their characters. Chuck Martin was quite prolific, having written for many Western magazines besides *Wild West Weekly*. In 1929 he made fifteen hundred dollars a month.[31] Martin literally lived the life of a true cowboy, having grown up on a few California ranches, and claimed he knew Wyatt Earp and the Daltons. On his ranch, or "Boot Hill Rancho," as his stationery called it, Chuck built his own "Literary Boothill," a private cemetery where he laid to rest the characters he killed off in his stories. He was proud of it, and more than willing to take visitors on a tour when they were in the area. The magazine was proud of it too, and featured it at least once in "A Chat with the Range Boss."

The heroes were the backbone of *Wild West Weekly*, but readers' letters were the pulse. Letters to the editor were always important for pulp magazines, because many times they were the only clue the publisher had as to the nature of the magazine's readership. They helped the editor gauge what the readers wanted in their stories and how they wanted their heroes to behave. Just like ordering a sandwich in a deli, once a reader asked for more stories about a certain hero, it was the editor's and writers' duty to serve it up.

In the early years, letters from readers were included in "Wrangler's Corner" and then in "A Chat with the Range Boss," but later the letters were given their own column, "Readers' Branding Irons." Many of the letter writers, using some of the colorful vocabulary in the stories, declared a fervid allegiance to their favorite heroes:

Dear Range Boss:

Unbuckle your gun belt, sky your paws, and listen to this letter! Sonny Tabor's stories shore are humdingers. Kid Wolf, the Oklahoma Kid, and Johnny Forty-five are swell hombres.

George Krumm ought to turn in his badge, join up with Buck Foster, and start raising sheep. "Yores truly Buck Foster" is a champion sheep-herder. Yes, sir, he shore knows his woollies!

By heifers, Boss, where did you round up all the gun-slingin waddies who make 3w such a humdinger?

It would be plumb bueno with me if Sonny Tabor was put on the screen, with Bob Steele or John Wayne in the leading role. I think the other readin' hombres would like it too.

Keep the gals out of your magazine—they only spoil things. Tell all the waddies that I said "hello" and that I'm wishing them a lot of luck.

Yours till Sonny Tabor is hanged.

Bud the Kid
Barton, Ohio[32]

The subject that seemed to generate more controversy and more headaches for the editors was women's role in the stories. The appearance of a young, impressionable girl who had the audacity not only to have a *crush* on a hero but to *speak* to him would create an uproar.

The following fan letter from Bob Stratton, who was famous for his vehement objections to women in the stories, epitomizes the opinion:

Beef Department: Sonny Tabor was doing OK as an outlaw, he was alright as a Ranger, he is doing good as an undercover man now. But WHY Rita Meredith? When he met up with a gal named Goldie in "Errand of Justice," that was bad enough. But when he has a calico steady, that's awful! How about letting her get blown up by dynamite or fall off a cliff?[33]

However, a letter like this would often initiate a stream of objections from other readers, defending women and citing their important role in the settling of the West and their value as Americans.

All in all, *Wild West Weekly* was a good little workhorse for Street & Smith—a "staunch little magazine," as W. Henry Ralston, the company's vice president, called it—even though the *Weekly* would always be overshadowed by Street & Smith's more popular pulp, *Western Story Magazine.*[34]

After considerable research and effort by many people, it was determined that between 1928 and 1943, Grandpa wrote more than 440 stories for *Wild West Weekly*. As part of the Street & Smith machine, my grandfather's stories entertained tens of thousands, if not hundreds of thousands, of readers across the country. His stories are quick-moving Westerns with an optimistic tone and cheery dialogue—the classic bang-bang Western we think of when we think of depression-era adventures. They had a sense of innocence about them, probably one of the last times that the Western genre would be so inclined. Nothing could stop Grandpa's heroes from accomplishing their jobs, no matter what the odds, and they were much loved as a result. The vast majority of letters to the *Wild West Weekly* editor clamored for more Sonny Tabor stories, more Kid Wolf adventures, more Johnny Forty-five with his clumsy and irritating sidekick.

The Street & Smith bookkeeping records also revealed that my grandfather had made a lot of money. While millions went hungry and homeless during the Great Depression, my grandfather made a princely average of four hundred to five hundred dollars a month, almost four times the national average.

Grandpa's novel had been a poor seller. If history judges writers on the number of books sold, my grandfather will be deemed a failure. But during the depression, when millions of people bought, read, and depended on pulps for entertainment when nothing else was affordable, he was a vital part of their lives.

Three days after arriving in Los Angeles for the summer, I drove to Arizona to meet Grandpa's half brother, George, and half sister, Phyllis. George had been delighted when I had e-mailed him that spring. He had lost touch with his brother years before he died. Come to Phoenix, he said, and we'll talk.

There couldn't have been two brothers so disparate in

looks, temperament, lifestyle, history, and outlook. Grandpa was short and paunchy from drinking. George, even though slightly stooped now with age, is tall and wiry, fit from swimming every day. Grandpa had the soft face of his mother, George the angular face of his father. Grandpa, from what I knew, was erratic, moody, and withdrawn, George jovial and gregarious. Grandpa dropped out of high school and resisted everything his father suggested, while George followed in his father's footsteps and became a psychiatrist. I look at George and I see a life full of patience and hard work, full of accomplishments, travel, and family. A life so different from Grandpa and Mary's, which I had always imagined as dark, like their house in Oakland: full of grays and browns, melancholy and fractured by disappointment.

But this weekend, George and Phyllis remembered their brother fondly. The binges, the borrowing of money, the long years of silence are still there. But for this weekend, Paul Powers the drunk is pushed aside and Paul Powers the pulp writer is celebrated. George pulled out several issues of *Wild West Weekly* that he had kept for sixty years. He had a pile of book reviews after *Doc Dillahay* was published. He pulled out photos; we laugh at one of Grandpa standing haughtily wearing ridiculous woolly chaps, the type worn by the early B-Western stars. The chaps still hang on the family room wall at the home of George's son Jerry.

George had helped Grandpa out financially in the years after *Doc Dillahay* was published. Still, they lost contact in the early 1960s after my father died.

George asked how Paul died. I had a copy of his death certificate and pulled it out for George to see. Quietly, solemnly, he looked at it. "Subdural hematoma. Head injury." He looked at it a long time without saying anything more.

The street in Garden Grove on which my aunt Pat and her husband live is hidden behind the strip malls of a busy boulevard. Yet the street is quiet and has a rural feel; there are no sidewalks here, and large trees flank each end of the block. I pull up to a well-tended two-story house with an English garden. Suddenly I feel as if I'm in the southern California I'd visited as a child.

And there is Pat, standing at her front door. She has the same serene smile that belonged to her mother. As I walk up to greet her, nothing else in my search matters as much as that moment.

We spent all afternoon sifting through papers in the two containers. There was so much of it, I decided to just sort for now. Any reading would have to wait until later.

I picked up a folded gray piece of paper. The letterhead was from *Wild West Weekly*, Street & Smith publishers, 79 Seventh Avenue, New York NY. Dated January 16, 1934, and addressed to Paul Powers, Portal, Arizona, it began, "We were pleased to purchase the Sonny Tabor novelette . . ."[35]

Both boxes were full of the small gray notes, all letters from Street & Smith, some with their envelopes still stapled to them. Most of them seemed to be from the 1930s, with a few from the 1940s. Always formally addressed to Mr. Paul Powers, always at a different address. God, the addresses. How many are there, I thought. It seemed that there was a different address for every year, some years two or three. 1930, Long Beach; 1931, Flagstaff; 1932, Tucson; 1936, Santa Fe; 1937, Laguna Beach; 1938, El Cajon.

"I remember sometimes we moved in the middle of the night," Pat said. "We even had to leave our own personal stuff. You know, like dishes, lamps, anything we had bought while we were there. My mother would protest, but my father would just say 'Don't worry about it! We can always buy more. I'll always make enough money.'"[36]

Her father never revealed his reasons for uprooting them so often and so abruptly. Houses were always rented; Grandpa didn't want to be tied down to a piece of real estate, and he always rented furnished so their transitions could be as effortless as possible, just like his pulp Western characters, wandering across the Southwest in some kind of timeless dimension. While other people starved during the depression, Grandpa moved.

I kept pulling out the little gray letters, all written by a Mr. Ronald Oliphant, Editor. A pattern emerged: Oliphant always asking Grandpa when he could expect more work from him, complaining when he hadn't heard from him for weeks at a time, wondering when he'll receive a story that was promised a week before. "We are not getting anything like enough stories about Kid Wolf and Sonny Tabor. We particularly need a 12,000 word Sonny Tabor novelette for an issue that is to go to press the week of April 6th, but the cupboard is bare."[37] There seemed to be hundreds of other letters, typed manuscripts, receipts, articles, ledgers, torn pieces of paper, manuscripts shoved into envelopes. Some fan letters from readers of *Wild West Weekly*. The *Doc Dillahay* galleys. Dozens of letters from its publisher, the Macmillan Company. Bills, scribbled notes, pages half full of a short story that never got past the first two paragraphs.

How ironic. After a lifetime of having almost zero information about him, I confronted mountains of minutiae.

"He kept everything!" Pat said, amused. She held up a shopping list.

Toward the bottom of the container I found a manila envelope, much like the other ones. I opened it.

Pulp Writer: Twenty Years in the American Grub Street.

I looked through it quickly. It was roughly 160 pages. I clutched it, disbelieving. This was more than I ever expected, ever dreamed of getting.

I'd found the lost life of my grandfather.

Pulp Writer

Twenty Years in the
American Grub Street

PAUL S. POWERS

To Ronald Oliphant,
a friendly critic
and to Bennett MacDonald,
an uncritical friend

CHAPTER 1

I'd Write a Mile

3. (*preceding page*) Paul posing during his early pulp-writing days. Probably taken in Nogales or Bisbee, Arizona, in 1931. On the back of the photo, he wrote, "An Arizona desperado." *Photo by Mary Powers.*

Something more than twenty years ago, when I was seventeen, my first story was sold to a magazine, but I suppose my first "professional" writing was done when I was a freshman in high school, several years before then. My word rate was one package of cigarettes per thousand words. Nor did I consider myself underpaid. Cigarettes were illegal in Kansas at that time, and not only for minors. They were sold, not too furtively, at from a quarter to thirty-five cents a pack. But then, they tasted better then—at least to me—than now; and back in those days the writing, too, was much more fun. With caution, and I *had* to be cautious to the extent of chewing Sen-Sen, my fee for one theme or composition would last me throughout the week. Horace Jones, my only client, was the son of a prosperous wheat farmer and was well supplied with pocket money, so I wasn't much troubled by conscience. He was a football star, which I was not, and I suppose I should have written his class work simply for the glory. Even then I believed that if an author's work was worth anything at all, it was worth paying for. So Horace, with reluctance, came through.

One noon when I was at my desk reading Dana's *Two Years before the Mast*—the only interesting book in the school's dry and scanty library—Horace came along the aisle, paused with menace, and finally thrust a paper before me. I recognized my work, though it had been painstakingly copied in my friend's round handwriting; it had been corrected and graded by Miss Fisher, the English teacher, and I could smell something more sulfurous than cigarette smoke. It was

55

graded C minus. In trying to get Horace a C, or perhaps a C plus, I had been cutting things a bit too fine.

"Well, what have you got to say about that?" he accused.

"It's passing, isn't it?"

"It ain't much more. What do you think I've been giving you all those Camels for?" Horace complained, not unreasonably. He had lowered his voice, and now he pushed into the seat beside me. "You can do a lot better than that."

"Sure I can. But if I made 'em too good, Fisher would know you didn't write 'em." I was brutally frank about it. "Don't you see that's so? If you'd had me do these things right from the first of the semester it might be different, but if you improved *too* fast she'd be sure to get wise."

Horace thought for a while, and at last admitted that I was probably right. After that, things progressed smoothly enough until toward the end of the term, when the time came for him to hand in his three required book reviews. When it was gently hinted that the word rate would now be somewhat advanced, Horace bleated disapproval.

"*Four* packs? Why, I was going to give you two—considering you got more employment, you ought to take less. You know I'll flunk out if I don't get those reviews in by Wednesday, and you're chislin' on me, that's what you're doing! You wait until school's out," he threatened darkly.

"Next year there'll be English II," was my reminder.

Horace paled under his acne, but he still wasn't ready to surrender. "Now, you listen here, Powers! I'll get somebody else to do these for me. Jim Doyle would do it for two packs."

"I guess he would. But does he know just what Fisher expects from you, like I do? If you want to take the chance, all right. But my price is four packs."

I got my four packs.

Now, I haven't reported the above merely to ridicule Horace Jones, who was not stupid, but simply had as much trouble with English composition as I was having, at the same time, with algebra and geometry. In hiring someone to help him he was smarter than I was, for he passed through the four years of high school and received his diploma. That was more than I could do.

This partnership with Horace Jones should have warned me that I was doomed to become a pulp writer (or, much worse, a "ghost writer"), for the setup was one that has confronted me, in one way or another, ever since. Let Miss Fisher represent the public, and Horace the editor who is trying to please her. A pulp writer must write well, but must not overdo it or he will get his editor into trouble with his readers. In asking for payment he should have some gumption, and not work too cheaply, for if he accepts "two packs" he will soon find himself toiling for "one pack" or for single cigarettes only. But he mustn't ask more than his Horace can afford to pay. If I had asked my employer for an entire carton he would have rebelled and, I suppose, employed Jim Doyle, who could have done the job as well as or better than myself anyway.

And it must be remembered that Horace, the middleman in this deal with the austere Miss Fisher, was the gainer in the long run. The editor—or it might be better to say, the publisher—is usually the winner in these games, and of course he should be. Like Horace, they know what they want to do, and are willing to pay, not ungenerously, to have it done for them. I am not soured on this pulp writing business, nor have I any reason to be. Under my own name, but usually under the several pen names I have used, more millions of words have been published than I care at the moment to tote up. I have been paid, by one company alone, in the neighborhood of one hundred thousand dollars. It's this writer's intention to tell, to the best of his ability, how it was done.

This book will be one of very personal experience, and not in any sense a textbook on the art of fiction writing. In my opinion, too many of them have been published already.

Many have written more for the pulps, and more ably, than I have. To mention only three, and not necessarily in the order of their productiveness: H. Bedford Jones, Walt Coburn, and Frank Richardson Pierce. Some of these, and others among the pulp mighty, also write for the "slicks." If any working pulp writer were to write a textbook it should be one of these—my twenty years make me only a brash newcomer to the game.

Well, what *is* a pulp writer? someone might ask. A pulp writer is one who earns his living by writing for the pulp magazines, which are those brightly covered periodicals that cover the newsstands in such dazzling profusion: magazines dealing with love, with Western adventure, with detectives, with pseudoscientific fiction, with most anything, all printed on uncoated paper similar to that of your newspaper, and selling from ten to twenty-five cents a copy. Those are the pulps. Who supplies all that material? Who edits them? Who reads them?

Answering the last question first, I can only say that the pulp "public" is very large and surprisingly variegated. General Dwight D. Eisenhower, for instance, is said to be an avid reader of Westerns, yet I could hardly call him a typical one. And Theodore Dreiser was once a pulp editor. I don't think he liked it much.

Is a pulp writer the same as a hack writer? Sometimes, but there are hack writers in the slicks too. Many of the present-day big names got their start in the pulps. Some are proud of having fought their way up, and others, curiously enough, are a little bit ashamed of their past. For instance, Mr. Rex Stout took some radio time, not long ago, to vigorously deny the German propaganda accusation that he had begun his literary career in this underhanded manner. Mr. Stout assured his listeners—here and in Germany—that he wasn't, and never had been, a pulp writer. Of all the vile falsehoods that came out of the Axis camp, that one seemed to get under the skin of Mr. Stout most painfully.

For a contrast, during a correspondence regarding some work I had done with—believe it or not—a Russian cowboy who had been made the hero of some Western stories, Dorothy Ducas of the Office of War Information's magazine division informed me that "Mr. Elmer Davis had written pulp stories himself a long time ago." I was very glad to know that Mr. Davis wasn't especially worried about living it down.

One thing can be said for the pulp magazines, whether for or against according to the point of view: I believe they are more thoroughly read, once bought, than such publications as the *Saturday Evening Post* or *Collier's*. Although the pulps have no pictures to attract the eye, no beautifully printed advertisements, they are literally read to pieces. The usual buyer of a slick paper magazine looks through it, reads maybe one article or story, and puts it aside. The contents are so diversified that the purchaser is bound to find something that will interest him, but he will hardly want to read it from cover to cover. It is otherwise with the pulps. The magazines are usually *all* Westerns, *all* mystery, *all* sports, and the "fan" drinks up every word of them. The writer for the pulps needn't worry, anyhow, that his work won't be read. It will be thoroughly criticized too! The author must continually watch his step, and an error or even the semblance of an error will be immediately spotted by the clientele. The readers of pseudoscience and of sports are particularly keen witted, and the writer of a Western story who makes a mistake in the caliber, rotation motion, or trajectory of a Winchester rifle bullet will, before the storm of disapproval has subsided, feel like using one of the bullets on himself. One fan of Westerns wrote me a scalding letter regarding the color of the smoke of a black-powder cartridge charge when seen against a twilight background of snow. Another writer for the same magazine received a protest from a native of Mozambique, East Africa, when he caused his stage-driver hero to leave his team standing in the street unattended.

The pulp magazines vary in literary quality. Some—for example, *Adventure* and *Argosy*—print very good fiction indeed, and have been represented in short-story anthologies. Their writers are more expert workmen than many who appear in the "highbrow" publications, and they often make more money. A pulp writer with an income of from ten to twenty thousand dollars a year isn't much bothered by the sneers of the "arty" group. Even a five-thousand-dollar emolument, in normal times, will keep the writer's doorway clear of furbearing animals. No matter what an author's literary ambitions are, or how high they may soar, he must usually support himself and his family; and, while he is learning his profession—a course of study that usually requires many years—I know of no trade that will offer him a better living.

Some of the pulps, I shall be the first to admit, are pretty terrible. Usually these odoriferous ones are thrown upon the newsstands by unscrupulous, fly-by-night publishers who are out to cheat their writers as well as the public. In any case, they usually fold up after an issue or two.

The writer for the pulps has the same choice the readers have—he can try his hand at just one particular type of magazine writing, that of scientific adventure of the Jules Verne–Buck Rodgers school, for instance, and specialize in that; or he may want to diversify in several fields and write sea stories, let us say, or fiction dealing with aviation and its sidelines. The pulp periodicals cover almost everything—in a ghastly manner sometimes, but they cover it. I think there's even a *Death Ray Monthly* on the market. If there isn't, there should be. And *Fiendish Stories*, the contents of which, I fear, would be pretty mild. The would-be pulp writer can pay his money—for postage stamps—and he can take his choice.

Considering the increase of population, it doesn't seem that the pulps are quite so popular as twenty years ago, though without a doubt they are here to stay, for better or worse. The "comic books"—which are compilations of the old-fashioned "funny paper" in tabloid size—have made inroads, especially among the youngsters of teen age who used to have enough mental energy to read, at least. To answer this "menace," most of the pulp companies have been publishing comic books of their own, and sometimes they are drawn from fiction characters popularized in the straight magazines owned by the firm; some of my own creations have appeared in that manner. I'm not kicking at the comic books; Donald Duck and his friends are the most delightfully humorous characters of our time, and have been favorites of mine since Walt Disney first conceived them. There are, of course, comic books *and* comic books.

In the 1920s there were certainly fewer of these pulp paper magazines, and I believe that, on the whole, they were of better quality. It's not so very difficult to sell a story today; hundreds are doing it, and one out of every three people I meet, these days, greets me with "I hear you're a writer; I've got a cousin who does a lot of writing; sells it too; his (or her) name is so-and-so; ever hear of him (or her)?" Usually I have to answer that I haven't. But then, very few people have ever heard of me either. As I said, it's not hard to sell an occasional story. The difficult thing is selling your work consistently enough to make a living out of it.

I'm a book collector by hobby, and while browsing through a dusty shop not long ago I picked up a copy of *Workers of the Nation*, published in two volumes in 1903. It was purchased because it was cheap and had a beautiful colored plate by Frederic Remington, and it was not until later that I discovered that the book was interesting in itself, being a comprehensive survey of all occupations as there were at the turn of the century. The chapter titled "Literature and Allied Professions" was especially informative, and I quote from it:

An author states that he once asked a veteran and accomplished writer for the press, who won a reputation by his first book, and has since contributed for fifty years to most of the leading reviews and magazines of the United States: "How much money can a man with a first-rate constitution, and with the very best education which America and Europe united can give, earn yearly by writing for periodicals? Can he earn $2,000?"

"No."

"Can he earn $1,600?"

After some thought he replied: "Yes; but that is all." "An industrious writer," says a novelist, "by the legitimate exercise of his calling, can just exist, no more. No man should enter on the literary life unless he has a fortune or can live contentedly on $2,000 a year. The best way is to make a fortune first and write afterward."[1]

That's how it was, according to this book, forty years ago. It's pretty evident that there was no pulp magazine market in those days! But then, a writer with "the very best education which America and Europe united could give" would, in all likelihood, turn up his distinguished snoot at anything so crude and vulgar had that opportunity been open to him. In those times, most aspiring authors wanted to write like Henry James. "Yes, and nowadays," one of my editor friends might say, "they want to *act* like Jesse."

There is much else in "Literature and Allied Professions" that seems naive to us today. Here are a few high spots from here and there throughout the chapter:

Poetry has long ago ceased to hold a place among the paying arts. . . . Edmund Clarence Stedman finds time to write poetry simply because of the revenue from his banking business. . . . Certain it is that today a man cannot live by poetry alone. He must either write prose five and a half days a week, devoting himself to poetry only on Saturday afternoons and Sundays, or else engage in

some kind of business or other prosaic pursuit in order
that he may earn a livelihood.[2]

Many poets of today would agree with that, maybe; and yet
how about such bards as Newman Levy, Samuel Hoffenstein,
and others too numerous to mention who seem to have done
quite well without having to restrict themselves to Sundays
and Saturday afternoons? Of course, a poet can always get a
job as a Librarian of Congress, so I wouldn't paint the picture
too darkly for present-day versifiers.

To continue:

That some exceedingly inferior writers do succeed
amazingly is a fact that cannot be denied. Their success,
however, is due either to the fact that they have paid
well for the éclat of a well-advertised name—assuming
the heavy risk of manufacturing and publishing their
first efforts—or else that they have cultivated the friendship of some complacent editor or publisher, willing to
rate the feeble output of a friend at least as highly as
the finished products of a stranger. Whether the last result always follows or not, no person with literary ambitions can dispense with the numerous professional ad-
vantages derived from forming friendly relations with
editors and publishers. . . . Even if his home is far from
the great publishing centers, the wise story writer finds
it worth the cost of the railroad journey to New York,
Boston, Philadelphia, Chicago or San Francisco to call
upon the editors.[3]

Let me say now, that if this were ever true, which I doubt,
it is certainly not necessary nowadays. I've never heard of
anyone selling a story through pull, or because he was a
brother-in-law of the editor. It might happen sometimes,
but the editor who allowed his personal feelings to influ-

ence his judgment would be collecting on his unemployment insurance. I have never in my life *met* an editor, not even the one who shares the dedication of this book. A writer's work speaks for itself, and so far as I know, the publishers don't care what color of hair their writers have, or whether they have any at all. I detest apple-polishing, and one of the things that I've liked about the writing game is that I've never had to do any bowing or scraping in order to get fair consideration for my work. Unless, through correspondence with him over a period of time, I found that I liked the man, I wouldn't go across the street to see an editor. Editors are busy men, and it's my work they want to see, I hope, and not me.

I know of no job that's a bed or roses exactly, unless it's horticulture, and in the following pages I shall tell of some of my own experiences, up to now. Writing in the third person, through all these years, it's seldom I get to use that fourth key on the right side of the third bank of my typewriter. But as you've already discovered, I know where it is.

With the radio and the cinema to write for, aspiring authors may not be looking toward the lowly pulps in these latter days, but if any are, they can read my humble saga and take warning, or encouragement, according to their temperaments. I won't, God helping me, become cynical in the telling. I know, from bitter experience, that the sufferings of unrequited authorship are very real, and that only the agonies of a young man in love can be compared to them.

Fortunately, the one with the urge to write at least knows what he wants and should, at least, know how to go about getting it. All he needs, if he has some talent, is a supply of guts. Or, as the vulgar would put it, intestinal fortitude. He will need more persistent, stubborn courage than in any other profession that I am acquainted with. He must be a glutton for punishment, but if he learns to *like* punishment, he's sunk. If each rejection slip makes him mad enough to sit down and write another story, and he gets a little madder and works a little harder after each refusal—then he's got a good chance to win through. Now, all this has been said before and said better. I hate platitudes, anyhow. From now on, I'm going to tell just what happened to *me*.

CHAPTER 2

King of the Photoplay;
And I Write a Joke

4. Family portrait, ca. 1909. Dr. John Harold Powers, Grace Powers, sister Nell, and Paul. *Collection of Patricia Binkley.*

Attending high school, a class ahead, was a young man much admired by me. As in the case of Horace Jones, I shall here give a name that resembles his true one—Dick Weaver is close enough. We would pitch horseshoes at his place after school, or play catch, and he had a book on "How to Put the Shot." Dick had bought a sixteen-pound lead ball (four pounds too heavy for kids of our age), and he was out after the record held at that time, I think, by Ralph Rose. All he had to do was "put" it three inches farther every week, and in about three years he would be world's champion. For some reason, I don't believe it worked out, although I am still muscle-bound from practicing with him. He also had a course in wrestling written by one Farmer Burns. It described Joe Stetcher's method of applying a "body scissors" to a sack of bran with such power as to burst it open. Although Dick didn't quite succeed with the sack of bran, I still regretfully remember the method. And besides being an enthusiastic disciple of Charles Atlas and Lionel Strongfort, Dick was not one to neglect the higher intellectual life. One day he had something new to show me.

"What is it, Dick?" He not only had a room of his own, but an entire suite of them at a rickety end of the house, and among his treasures were a desk, an old filing cabinet, and an ancient typewriter.

"Photoplay writing," he said and I quote. "Turn off that gramophone."

I was more interested in Dick's Edison phonograph than in his typing machine. Did you ever hear "Laska" recited on one of those old cylinder records, "Laska . . . down by the

Rio Grande"? If you haven't then you've missed something. You would weep just as much after the tenth playing as you did the first time, and maybe a little more. Among Dick's music was "Red Wing," rather nasal and far away, but a nifty. Then there was a minstrel record: "There was three—or was it four?—men floatin' down the river on a marble slab; one of the men was blind and couldn't see; one of the men didn't have no arms; and the other man didn't have no clothes on. Well, the man that was blind, he seen a duck; the man that didn't have no arms, he picked up a gun and shot the duck; he handed it to the man that didn't have no clothes on, and *he* put it in his pocket." Dick and I always laughed immoderately at this story and its denouement. I thought it was funny then. I still think so.

"I'm writing my first photoplay—a story for the motion pictures," Dick disclosed.

I was dazzled, and was even more impressed when Dick showed me the "course" he had paid, I think, about fifty dollars for. There was a portfolio packed with glossy lesson sheets, but the most interesting item was a large page in full color that reproduced dozens of checks ranging in amount from five hundred to five thousand dollars, all having been paid, presumably, to scenario writers. The names of various picture studios were on the checks, and they looked—and probably were—authentic. As late as 1922 and probably later, the young movie industry did buy original stories from "unknowns." Dick really might have had something there, and it is to be regretted that he and possible opportunity didn't come into collision a few years later when he was more mature. Anyhow, it looked good, although I was unable to make anything out of the same scenario that the course included. It ran along something like this:

Scene 55—Ravensdale running along top of freight
    train, closely pursued by masked men, who flour-
    ish guns.

Scene 56—Interior of caboose. Pauline, bound and
gagged, is shown struggling in her bonds. Caboose door shown opening slowly.
Scene 57—Close-up of Jack Craig's brutal face in doorway; he sneers evilly. Subtitle—"At last, girl, I have
you in my power. You cannot escape. Marry me, or
. . ."
Scene 58—Ravensdale reaches top of caboose, drops
to platform, throws open caboose door.
Scene 59—Close-up of Ravensdale's face registering
fury. Subtitle—"Take your vile hands off my bride-
to-be, Jack Craig!"

"I can't figure all this out," I had to admit after reading
half a dozen pages of the same.

"You've got to have imagination," Dick said. "Why, I can
close my eyes and see that whole thing. I've already got nineteen pages of my own scenario written up. According to the
Acme School of the Photoplay, I can't expect more than five
hundred dollars for my first scenario. They say that's what
they usually pay beginners, but I think I've got a way figured
so they'll pay me two thousand or maybe three thousand."

Every afternoon for a week or more after that I was at Dick's
house, watching the progress of the masterwork that was to
bring fortune, and perhaps fame, to Dick Weaver; and I was
almost as confident of his success as he was himself. With the
sample scenario was a brief synopsis of the play, which ended
somewhat as follows:

After the wedding in the death cell, Ravensdale is taken
to the scaffold and hanged—almost.

"Lesson Number Twenty says that's to arouse the movie
studio editor's interest," Dick explained patiently. "Ravensdale doesn't get hung in 'The Stolen Pearls,' you know that.

But the studio editor wouldn't know, and he's got to read the scenario to find out. That way, he'd be more likely to buy it, the Lesson says. Here's how I ended *my* synopsis." And I read:

> After the gory demise of Demon Clayton, Frank marries Pauline, but the happy pair are captured on their way out of the church and shot—almost.

"Isn't that quite a lot like the other one?"

"It's nothing at all like the other one," Dick said, rather irritated. "Now here's the letter I'm going to send along with the photoplay and synopsis. When they read it, they won't be so apt to think this is my first scenario."

The carefully typed note was brief, modestly phrased, but it ended in a sentence full of quiet triumph: "This is the best photoplay I have put out in my career."

The story was duly mailed, while Dick made plans to buy a motorcycle—"or maybe an automobile." Several weeks elapsed, and one day he told me, with some dismay, that the film epic had been returned without comment. It was sent out several times again, but for some strange reason it was not accepted, and sometimes the thick envelope was returned unopened. After a while, Dick grew tired of sending it out, and I don't think he ever attempted another "picture play."

Now there was nothing absurd about Dick's effort. He was discouraged too easily. The movie studios do not consider stories submitted in that way today, but I still believe that if Dick had stuck tenaciously enough to the writing business he might have succeeded. Stranger things have happened.

I never took a "course" myself in any kind of "Learn to Write for Publication" study, by correspondence or otherwise. I'm neutral on the subject. I've met a pulp writer or two who admitted that he had been helped by such courses, but when I first started out I was too poor to take one, and since then I've been too busy.

Dick's experience, even though it hadn't worked out successfully, set me to thinking. I knew I didn't have the wits to construct a scenario, even with the help of the Acme School of the Photoplay, but I knew that magazines bought stories—they *had* to, or where would they get them?—and there didn't seem to be anything very mysterious about the writing of a short story. Fiction would be much easier, or so I imagined, than the crazy jargon of a movie script. Why couldn't I write some stories? In a small ad in some cheap magazine I was reminded that Jack London, or somebody, received thirteen hundred dollars for just one short one. An evening's work! Of course, I would be willing to start at the bottom, and only a small part of that four-figure amount would suit me, at least in the beginning. I'd always been writing things, since away back in the fourth and fifth grades. Many a notebook had been filled with my stories of adventure, all illustrated by myself. I would need a typewriter, of course, and soon had permission to use the Underwood Number Four which sat, seldom used, in the business office of the hospital.

I lived in a central Kansas town of about seven hundred population, where my father was physician and surgeon. The place was in some ways forward-looking and progressive, as Main Street was brick-paved, and it had a city water supply and electricity. There was also a modern hotel, and a hospital had been built, but there was no public library. Even smaller communities in the vicinity had taken advantage of Mr. Carnegie's philanthropy, but ours wasn't a bookish town. I had been born here, but had spent five formative years away in Winfield, Kansas, and later in Pueblo, Colorado. Being used to books, I felt starved for them when I had returned with my family in 1915. In the meantime I had forever lost the best teacher I could have, or hope to have—my mother. The love of books had been implanted in me, thanks to her, way back at the beginnings of memory.

This was one reason—there were others—why the people of the town considered me something of a screwball. They thought I was a little "te'ched" when I went from house to house one summer and asked at each place if they had any books. And, if they had, could I borrow some? I'd bring them right back, I promised. Nobody ever turned me down, that I remember; it was a kindly town. But I don't believe there were more than a few wheelbarrowsful of books in the settlement. I made one find at the home of a Scotch storekeeper, and he was good enough to lend me what I wanted of his trove. He was sympathetic toward my love of reading, but he warned me that after once reading Robert Bur-r-r-rns I'd never be wanting to read anything else. "And why should ye?" was his fair enough question. Mr. Berwick was all right; but most of the town considered books as impractical foolishness.

I suspect that the three-hundred-odd volumes at our home was the largest collection of reading matter in the town, and my father's medical library, which he took care to keep up to date, was perhaps twice that size. Besides medical periodicals, we "took in," as the British say, the *Saturday Evening Post, American Magazine*, and *Literary Digest*. Kansas-born himself, my father was conservative in the little lay reading that he had time for. He was more pleased than otherwise at my determination to be a writer, although he thought I would change my mind long before I attained that goal. I suppose he hoped that this ambition of mine would be incentive enough to take me through high school and college; he believed that success of any kind, especially in this field, would be impossible without a formal education. As a writer, he reminded me, I would have to compete at every point with university men. He would have liked to have had me follow his own footsteps, but I think he understood as well as I did that while I was interested in the theoretical, imaginative side of his profession, I was unfitted for its practice. Fortunately, I left the medical career to my young half brother, who, in the navy at this writing, is no doubt gaining a comprehensive knowledge of Japanese anatomy.

One of my favorites among the books, the one that made the deepest impression on me, was Hugo's *Les Miserables*. I had read it first when I was about thirteen, and it took possession of me as no book had done before and few have since. Victor Hugo may not have had the somber power of Dostoyevsky and Tolstoy—no matter how hard he pushed, his probe didn't go as deeply into the human heart as theirs—but who can forget Fantine, little Cosette, and that supersoul, Jean Valjean? And Javert haunted my sleep. Melodrama, maybe, but what tremendous melodrama!

Long before Hugo, there had been the incomparable Horatio Alger. I also read some Oliver Optic, but couldn't long stomach his namby-pamby characters. One of them, I remember, was bawled out by a highly moral ship's captain for using the horrid expression, "Shiver my timbers!" Series of boy's books were in vogue too, in these almost movie-less days, and I preferred the *Pony Rider Boys* and the *Motor Boys* to the then already old-fashioned *Rovers*, but most exciting of all was Frank Merriwell.

To return to the typewriter. Neither I nor anyone else around the hospital knew much about manipulating one, and still less was known about its insides. My father's fountain pen took care of all the writing he had to do, and when I told him that there was something seriously wrong with the machine he was mildly surprised.

"I don't see how it could be worn out," he said. "It's never been used much."

When I showed him that the letters "e" and "o" were identical black spots, like oversized periods, and that the insides of the "b" and "p" characters were likewise solid, he suggested that I buy a new ribbon. But that made it worse. I experimented for a couple of days, I think, before I finally took a pin and lifted a little disk of impacted dirt and ink from the center of the "o." The only thing wrong with the typewriter was that it needed cleaning. Feeling as if a "new planet had swum into my ken," I got to work, using the same typing system I use today. One thing can be said for it: the ordinary typist would be terribly handicapped if by some accident his hands were mutilated, while I could suffer the loss of both thumbs and three fingers on each hand and type just as well as I do now. I recommend the system highly.

My first story was finally completed after about two weeks of painful work, during which I discovered that composition wasn't quite so easy as I had expected. Paragraphing and punctuation were especially perplexing, but not as important, perhaps, as I then thought. The length of paragraphs is more or less arbitrary, especially in the pulps, where editors often chop one into two or three to give the text the effect of more rapid movement. The semicolon, too, gave me needless trouble. One needn't use it at all. Short sentences can be balanced with long ones, and an ear for prose is soon developed. I'll admit the example is a bit extreme, but if punctuation ever bothers you, glance through James Joyce's *Ulysses.*

When the story was finished, I faced the problem of what to do with it. It may as well be said now as later that the yarn was never published, but just then my hopes were "ceiling unlimited." The manuscript was dispatched at once to some sort of a "Literary Bureau" that I had seen advertised in a magazine. That was a mistake, but fortunately I began to work on another story before hearing anything from the first one. This was addressed to another such bureau, and I swung into my third effort.

I had already blundered upon something of value. The beginning writer should always have more than one story in the mails, if only as a hedge against despair. A rejected manuscript, cold and pitilessly "as is," is an awful thing to contemplate, and it never reads as splendidly as it did when fresh from the typewriter. Unless the author has another script on its travels—always a better one, of course—he might not have the courage to go on.

In about two weeks I received a letter from the first "bureau," and I didn't have to study it long before deciding that I was dealing with a gyp. My work was praised to High Heaven, but I noted that my name and address was in lighter type than the body of the communication, as was the neat "$16.25," which they demanded "to cover costs of revising and preparing for publication" my outstanding short-story masterpiece. After thinking it over, I sent postage for my masterpiece's journey home.

Culturally stagnant as our town was, we had several outstanding personalities, and the most interesting of these was the spinster, Miss Baxter, who dared to do some thinking for herself. She was an expert photographer, a professional, and a woman photographer was almost unheard of in Kansas as recently as a few decades ago. She sold magazines and other oddments in her shop and studio on Main Street, and sometimes such publications as *Harper's* and *Scribner's* were on display, though I suspect that the only eyes to examine their innards were the keen ones behind the sparkling pince-nez of Miss Baxter herself. It was in the studio that I made my acquaintance with *Life* (the old humorous magazine, not the present *Life*), and *Judge*, before they found their way to the barbershop.

"This ought to interest you," Miss Baxter remarked dryly when I called one morning, and she handed me the first copy of a writer's magazine that I had ever seen. How she had guessed, I don't know, but she had taken the first fur-rug-and-buttocks photograph of me that had ever been made and had been mildly interested in me ever since. I had been close-mouthed, thus far, about my ambitions of authorship, but I rather shamefacedly accepted the magazine.

Studying it as I have studied few things before or since, I learned a great deal that was of value to a beginner. For many years I haven't read a copy of one of these periodicals; they seem amateurish to me now, and no doubt they are. By the time a pulp writer has become reasonably proficient at his trade, he has usually established contacts, and knows how and where to submit his offerings, but to a beginning writer these often-laughed-at publications are of great help. Not only was there a list of "markets," but I also learned something about the preparation of manuscripts. Astonishingly enough, they should be double-spaced! Stimulated by the knowledge that I could send my stories directly to the editors of the magazines, I made a new start. There were things other than fiction, too, at which a writer could try his hand. Not only were "articles" bought, but even jokes were in demand. I decided to attempt some of the latter, and while I was about it, try some humorous essays of under one thousand words, pieces known as "skits."

It was the day of the two-line joke, or gag, as they are dubbed nowadays. "She" made a simply devastating reply to something that "he" said, or vice versa; or "Brown" simply floored "Jones" with a witty comeback. Although two lines were enough, they sometimes ran to five or six, and indeed it was best to include a few of these longer ones, as the newspapers used jokes as "fillers" to close up spaces of varying sizes. Sometimes a joke was written down in brief narrative form, but for the most part they were simply dialogue. The first joke I ever wrote, which of course never sold, was something like this:

CARELESS OF HIM

Mr.: (Sleepily)—Ah! The dawn is breaking.

Mrs.: That was only the milkman, dropping another bottle.

They were that terrible. Yet somewhere among all the rubbish I sent out were some gems of purest ray serene. There had to be, unless the law of averages counted for nothing. Typing each joke on a separate sheet of paper, with my name and address in an upper corner, I sent out batches almost daily to *Life*, *Judge*, and almost every magazine I had ever heard of. Whether they used jokes or not made little difference to me; I was confident they would soon be using them after they had seen mine. I also tackled every newspaper of any size in the country, not neglecting the nearby *Kansas City Star*. To save paper, I began cutting an 8½ x 11 sheet into three equal parts and typing a joke on each, and every batch was accompanied by a stamped, self-addressed envelope. In a notebook from a day-to-day I jotted down the number of jokes and where sent.

Then I began haunting the post office, and only the village imbecile watched the glass-fronted boxes more intently than I did at mail time. As our town was on a branch railroad, there were only two mail trains each day, and the arrival of the "passenger" eastbound in the morning and westbound at night was an event looked forward to by almost everyone. I was usually in the crowd that went down to see the train come in, for who could tell what dazzling news it might be bringing me? I breathlessly watched the unloading of the mail pouches, and followed them up into town, walking behind the two-wheeled handcart. Uncle Sam was now my middleman—my agent, so to speak. If an alienist had examined me at this time he would have said that I was in an "elated" state; later on I was to have delusions of grandeur.

When heavy envelopes filled with my humorous contributions began coming home to roost I was disappointed but not too disconsolate, as I felt that my efforts were improving, and there was always a more recent packet to pin my hopes upon. From *Life* I began receiving little "regret" slips, printed in green on yellow paper, but newspapers usually returned my offerings without even this attention. Finally, an envelope came back from the *Chicago Daily News* minus seven of my jokes. There was no accompanying letter, nothing whatever to indicate that there had been any acceptance. Examining my books, I found that I had indeed mailed twenty jokes. Only thirteen had come back, but wasn't it possible that the others might have been lost in the newspaper office?

A few evenings later, a small, thin envelope was dropped into the post office box that I had rented for my own. I got it open somehow—the words *Chicago Daily News* in the upper left-hand corner had given me paralysis agitans—and inside was a smeary black-printed payroll check: Pay to the Order of *Me!*—$3.50. I've received remittances since that were more than a hundred times as large, but none as electrifying as this one. I didn't realize it then, but I had sold my soul into bondage at that moment, sold it to a broadly smiling, very pleasant devil. Bless his heart! I tiptoed home on clouds.

CHAPTER 3

Art for the Artless

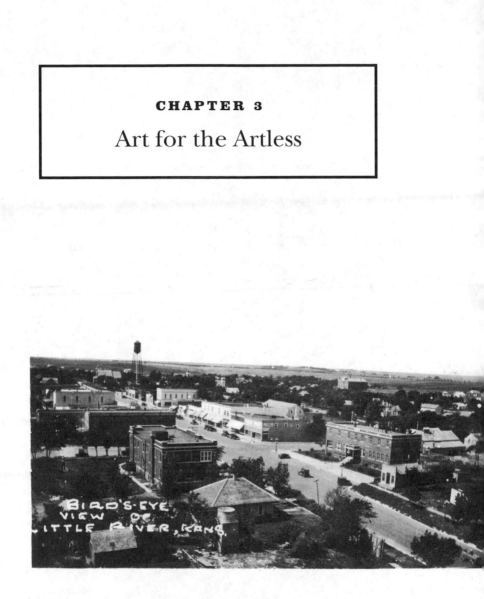

BIRD'S-EYE VIEW OF LITTLE RIVER, KANS.

5. Little River, Kansas, ca. 1916. After Paul's mother died, the family moved to Denver for a few years. Dr. Powers was asked to return to Little River to head a new hospital in nearby McPherson. *Author's collection.*

To the surprise of my family, but not to me, of course, my taste of success proved to be more than a fluke; if somebody in Chicago were making drunken mistakes, he remained in that besotted condition. A few days later, I was sent $6.50 for thirteen jokes, and these modest amounts continued to come. The checks were marked "Art Department," and when I succeeded in getting copies of the *News*, I found that each joke had been illustrated by a small pen-and-ink sketch, and these fillers appeared throughout the paper. Then I opened a return envelope from the *New York Sun* and found a check for two dollars inside in payment for two jokes. Eureka! This New York paper paid twice as much. I was still marveling over this when the *Chicago Herald and Examiner* began coming through. I received four or five checks at once from this publication, each for from one to three dollars. I didn't know it, but that paper had been running some sort of contest, and my jokes had been automatically entered in it. They paid me from six to twelve dollars a week until the competition was over; I would be sent up to eight small checks in one envelope, and it was the height of my glory to go from store to store, cashing them one at a time.

Our town held its annual agricultural fair that summer, and a group of newspapermen came from the not-distant city of Hutchinson for its opening. A local man was wanted to report the results of the three-day festival, and I consented to represent the *Gazette*, having already acted as correspondent for Mr. Paul Jones's *Lyon Daily News* nearby. But this experience as a reporter was my first—and last. I had to phone in my "news," and after nearly an hour's session in a baking-hot booth I was at the point of collapse, and had a great respect for newspaper "leg men." I could neither hear nor make myself heard, and I've had telephoniphobia ever since. In the garbled write-up, Mrs. Coover's prize bedspreads was printed "best breads" and the president of our WCTU took high honors with her "brandied cherries." For a while I thought I'd have to spend the *Gazette*'s four-dollar check for a ticket out of town. I distinctly said *candied* cherries. Or I think I did.

I continued the writing of short humorous bits, and my income fluctuated, but at this time it was around ten dollars per week. I was beginning to think I would never sell anything to *Life*, which was then America's foremost humorous publication, but one day I saw some penciled notations on one of my jokes, and I renewed my efforts. The pencilings were very cryptic, but it seemed to me that the piece had been voted upon. There were plus marks opposite two sets of initials, then a faint but decisive "No." Finally, I had an acceptance. An envelope of "returns" came with one joke removed, and in its place was a crisp, pinkish blue check for three dollars, signed, marvel upon marvel, by Charles Dana Gibson. It's unfortunate that I didn't save that check, for Mr. Gibson soon delegated the signing to others, and I believe that was the only check I received bearing his famous signature.

During this time I had been trying material of longer length, but without any success until Harry Stephen Keeler accepted two skits of about a thousand words each. In after years he became a successful writer of detective novels, but he was then editor of *Ten Story Book*, a not-too-successful Chicago publication. There was no check with the note of acceptance. For the first time, I was up against a "pay upon publication" plan. More than six months elapsed before the material was published, and I received my one cent per word as payment. My situation at this time was such that I could well afford to wait; I was in no great need of the money, and I was living in a golden haze anyway, waiting to see my name for the first time in a nationally circulated publication. In later years, when I was really a professional, with hungry mouths dependent upon my writing, I was to suffer through this ugly system of tying up an author's work, and farther on I shall have more to say about it.

When school resumed again that fall, I balked. By this time I should have been through high school, but I had flunked and kept flunking such things as algebra. Mathematics didn't interest me; I disliked it, and simply refused to waste my time on it. This probably indicates either a weakness of character or a lacuna in my mental makeup. It was probably both, but I have found that a talent in one direction very often is accompanied by a lack elsewhere. That's fair enough. We can't have everything—unless, of course, we are geniuses. To my father's disappointment, I announced that my formal education was finished, and no arguments would shake me. I've had occasion since to regret my mulishness, but I still feel that the education I dug out for myself was as good, in its way, as the one college would have given me.

Father agreed with *Workers of the Nation*, the book I quoted earlier, in that an author, to be in any way successful, should have the best education that America and Europe combined can offer. My small "flash in the pan" successes had surprised but not impressed him much; I believe it worried him a little. One day, however, something really caught his eye.

Someone on the editorial staff of the *Chicago Daily News* had been kind enough to send me some samples of material they were using on the editor's page, and I managed to sell them several brief humorous articles, some of them signed. One noon after lunch, Father parked himself in his easy chair for a few minutes' rest before returning to the hospital; he glanced through his *Literary Digest*, then removed the brown wrapper from that week's *Journal of the American Medical Association*. As was his habit before reading anything technical, he'd turn to "Tonics and Sedatives," the humorous column at the back of the book. I shall never forget his pride and pleasure when he saw a signed piece of mine there, reprinted with the permission of the *News*. I caused him so much worriment during his too short lifetime that I am prouder of that little piece today than of anything I've written since, although I have long since forgotten what it was about, except that it concerned doctors.

"Isn't there some school of writing we could send you to, Paul?" he meditated. "Seems to me that you might enroll as a special student in some university course."

We could find none, although I was eager to study at something so overpoweringly interesting as magazine writing. Then it occurred to Father that I might become an artist. I had always liked to draw, although quite untaught, and for my own amusement I had made many cartoons and comic sketches in India ink. Father had a better opinion of these than I did, and he felt that if I had training in art I might profitably combine my talents, and cartoonists, we had heard, made a great deal of money. Hearing of an art school in Denver, I sent a letter of inquiry, and it was soon decided that I should enroll later that month.

It wasn't until I was nearly ready to leave Kansas that I met Ben Wall, the first man I had met who could talk my own language. My senior by four or five years, he was working out of Salina for an implement company and preparing for a position in South America. I haven't seen him since that summer, but our conversations—sometimes held when we were jolting over country roads in his little car—are still well remembered. He was a poetry enthusiast, and I had only just discovered poetry. I had been in contact with it since childhood, but not until late adolescence did it take hold of me. That is the usual time, I suppose, but with me it was sudden. Blake's "Tiger, Tiger, burning bright" had, until then, seemed as inane and childish as Longfellow's "I shot an arrow into the air." Now I had become aware that Blake's bit of "sing-song" was of a high order of poetry. Mr. Longfellow remained about where he had always been, in my estimation, but I had been electrified by Keats, Shelly, and even some of Browning. Ben Wall introduced me to Housman's *Shropshire Lad* and to Masters's *Spoon River*.

I remember that I recited "The Harlot's House" one night, and I knew, too, much of the *Ballad of Reading Gaol* by heart. Ben wasn't responsive to Oscar Wilde.

"Don't you like 'The Harlot's House'?"

"I used to like Wilde," Ben said. "I ordered a complete set of his books from New York a couple of years ago. Then I sent them back, and insisted on the return of my money. I got it, too."

"What was wrong?"

"I found out that he was a sexual pervert," Ben said darkly.

"Are you sure about that?" I was shocked, because I didn't know, then, what Wilde had gone to "gaol" for.

Ben passed me the quart fruit jar full of home-brewed wine that he had got from one of his farmer clients. We took turns clamping it to our faces.

"It's a fact," Ben told me. "Walt Whitman was one too, and I won't read any of his poetry."

I thought a while. "There's a lot of Whitman I can't read," I admitted, "but how about *Out of the Cradle Endlessly Rocking* and *When Lilacs . . . ?*"

"I won't read any of him because of what he was," Ben said emphatically.

"It's the man's work you should judge, and not his character," I protested. "If a man writes beautifully I'm interested in his beautiful writing, and not especially in his sex life. What's that got to do with his poetry, even if he was the most immoral man on earth? Why, if you heard something against Edison's married life, you'd sit in the dark the rest of your life rather than turn on the lights he invented! Or would you?"

"Now, wait! Let me explain my position . . ."

He never did, of course, to my satisfaction, but that's a sample of the excited, immature talks we had. At that time such arguments seemed vastly important. Youth! Our ears were still ringing with the *Rubaiyat*, and we had a jar of wine between us in the cornfield wilderness. No wonder I have remembered Ben Wall.

Knowing nothing of the technical problems of versification, I wrote some poetry anyway. With admirable nerve, I mailed my verse to such places as the *Atlantic Monthly* and *Harper's*, as well as to the poetry magazines. My only acceptance was from the *Midwest Bookman*, published in Kansas City, and which tried desperately hard to be very, very lit'ry. But the joke on them turned out to be one on me.

When my piece was printed and I received the copies of the magazine that were sent in payment instead of money, I discovered that the last two lines of my verse, the ones that gave it meaning, had been omitted. It had been senseless enough in the first place, but without the point it was idiotic. In reply to my disgruntled letter, the lady replied that she was "heartsick about it. The printer and proofreader will be discharged."

I was afraid she meant it, and I hurried to urge her not to fire anyone on my account. The upshot of it was that several readers of the *Midwest Bookman* wrote in to praise my queerly mutilated verse. Maybe I could have established a new school of poetry. It never could have happened in the pulps; their readers aren't so naive.

Early in the autumn I established myself in Denver in a four-dollars-a-week room a few blocks from the golden-domed statehouse, and the world of Art was mine to conquer. Across Lincoln Street was the YMCA, but I chose not to stay there because it would have been more expensive unless I shared quarters with someone else, and I wanted the independence that "Bohemians" are supposed to find imperative. I think that I considered myself one. So that my time would be free for intense art study, Father sent me ten dollars a week to cover my expenses, but I rented a typewriter and counted upon at least doubling that income.

Denver wasn't exactly new to me; I had lived there during the winter of 1918 when the influenza had closed the schools, and I had spent many hours in the big, gray library in the civic center as well as in the State Historical Museum up the hill. Now acquaintance with both was pleasantly renewed. Denver seemed a roaringly big city after my years in a small town, but my dissipations were mild and consisted mainly of tickets to the Orpheum, for there was still vaudeville in those times, and the movies had yet to give it the coup de grâce. Down on Curtin Street, "Bozo," a putty-nosed comedian, was entertaining the lowbrows—including me—as only Bozo could; and here too was the famous Tabor Grand, recently changed to a cinema palace and prosaically renamed the Colorado. Speakeasies were getting under full steam.

The Denver School of Applied Art, near Trinity Church, was in the charge of Mr. Cory, the cartoonist for the *Denver Times*, who used a grease pencil somewhat in the manner of Fitzpatrick of the *St. Louis Post-Dispatch.* Cory was a great admirer of the Missouri artist, and I remember that his office was decorated with many Fitzpatrick originals.

On the first day I was admitted, without warning, to the life class where a young woman was posing in the nude. I was given a place in the circle of perhaps twenty students and, being provided with a large sheet of drawing paper, some sticks of charcoal, and a chamois skin, was told to give free rein to my talents, if any. Horribly embarrassed, I began work, noting out of the corner of my eye that about half the students were girls, and that a dazzlingly beautiful blonde was right at my elbow. I learned later that she was from Durango, a mining town in the southwest part of the state. What *she* wanted to draw for is something I still can't puzzle out.

In agony, I stole a look at the model and shakingly began making black lines on the paper. I hadn't expected anything like this, at least not in the very beginning. As there hadn't been a Presbyterian Church in our town, I had been sent to the Methodist Sunday School where I had learned very early that not only were dancing and card playing wrong, but that the unclad human body is particularly shameful. The model was making no attempt at concealment; she was, if I remember rightly, chewing gum with all the placidity of an animal ruminating its cud. And somehow, I had imagined that models used a depilatory. The works of art that I had seen certainly didn't reproduce all the details that now confronted me.

After about twenty minutes there was a rest period, during which the model, with a wrapper thrown loosely over her charms, circulated among us and casually inspected the students' interpretations while in the hallway a phonograph blared "Hot Lips." Nearly everyone lit cigarettes. A pretty fast crowd this, I thought, but of course I was mistaken; the school was as moral as a Barber's College.

It was my first experience with charcoal, a medium messy but expressive—if I'd had anything to express. The chamois skin would erase perfectly, and one could draw a line a dozen times without spoiling the surface of the paper. By working hard, and occasionally stealing a glance at the model, I managed to sketch in a figure that I thought very creditable. I continued dabbing at my creation, and feeling like a very devil, I detailed the breasts and drew in the nipples. Then I found myself elaborating the design into a sort of jeweled brassiere, and to the lower part of the figure I added panties. Why I did this, I don't know. Ask the Freudians.

During the next recess my work caused polite comment. "Interesting motif," one of the girls remarked (what a motif was I had no idea). "Rather Oriental," boomed a heavy-set student in his thirties. I'm sure they weren't laughing at me; my plight was too pitiful and evident for that. The instructor saw what I had done, but made no comment. Next day, however, when I again applied my fancy fig leaves (I was determined to clothe my picture decently in spite of the model's carelessness), he suggested something about my prospects of doing well in Mr. Cory's cartooning class. He was being sarcastic, I fear. At any rate, in a few days I managed to overcome my inhibitions to the extent of leaving my drawings in the raw. Of course, to an artist, what I have just said will seem stupid. Their eyes become as impersonal as those of a surgeon, and even more contemptuous.

What the teacher had said about entering the cartooning class appealed to me, and if it was a trap, I fell into it. As in my writing, I wanted quick results, and I still believed in get-successful-quick propositions. Mr. Cory granted me an interview. In a manner so pleasant that my suspicions should have been stirred, he told me that I might report downstairs to his class the next morning.

Pleased to know that I was to become a highly paid comic-strip artist right off the bat, I was on hand early and with an idea for a drawing I had mulled over during the night. Four others were in the advanced group, two of whom were commercial artists who hoped to enter a more lucrative field. I was shown to a desk and supplied with pens, pencils, ink, and bristol board. Mr. Cory smiled mildly at me and told me to go ahead with anything I had in mind.

My cartoon was meant to be something like the traffic safety pictures so common in these days, and among the objects in it, I remember, were a wrecked automobile, a tombstone, a human skull, and several people. Doing my very best, I toiled until nearly noon, and then I became conscious of a presence above and behind me. There was a deadly silence, suddenly shattered by a roar that rattled the windows and set the wall trembling.

Cory had the vocabulary of a mule skinner—plus the mule's. An army sergeant spreads out his abuse to cover your ancestors and immediate family, but Cory knew how to concentrate it, and his terrible tirade was directed at me alone. As it should have been. Omitting the sulphur: "Who told you, Powers, that you could draw? Look at the perspective! And what are those two-legged things? What the hell are they wearing? Stovepipe pants? You can't draw wrinkles in cloth like that! Don't you know anything at all about drapery? I've had six-year-olds sent to me from the kindergarten who could do better than this! And what's this stupid thing supposed to represent?"

"It's—a skull," I whispered.

"A skull! Well, for the love of my Creator! I thought it was a damned jack-o'-lantern! You've drawn a deformed pumpkin with holes in it at the wrong places. Did you ever see a skull? Did you ever see a skull that looks like *this?*"

"Yours does," I wanted to say. Oh, how I wanted to say it! And I still wish I'd said it. But I was too demoralized; my nerve, temporarily at least, was gone.

Mr. Cory continued. So I thought I didn't need training in the life class, did I? A cartoonist had to know his business from the ground up, and it took years, not days, to get the fundamentals, sometimes a lifetime. I could get to hell back to the life class and, by this and by that, I could damned well stay there until I had learned something. And I could go there right now, and quickly, or I could go on a longer journey, which would suit Mr. Cory just as well, anyhow.

Red with shame, I climbed the stairs to the life class. I think I went up on all fours.

Before many weeks I had decided to quit, once and forever, the study of art. Mr. Cory understood the artistic temperament and how to deal with it, but not even he could make anything out of mine. If my talents had been large enough I would have stuck it out, but, to treat myself kindly, my abilities were of the mediocre, or garden, variety. I came to the conclusion that I was going to become a writer, nothing else, and that I had best put in more time at it. Writing home to announce my new plans, I tried my hand at making a living for myself.

I wanted to write fiction, and did, but every short story came drifting back to me. There was never any encouragement, not even a penciled word on the rejection slips. It was now that I began the watchful waiting for the mail that has been my lot ever since. The postman, the writer's best friend and bitterest enemy! The heavy envelope used to land upon the hall table with a sickening plop, and sometimes there would be two or three. While in Denver I should have made it a point to call at the office of the *Author and Journalist* on Champa Street, for this trade magazine, edited and guide by Mr. Willard Hawkins, was one of the best in the country. Several years later I was to sell Hawkins an article, "How I Sold 10,000 Jokes," but then, as now, I was rather shy and conscious of myself.

Joke writing kept me more or less alive. I concocted an average of twenty a day, but only a few of these would be purchased, and I had many bad weeks when I would receive only two or three dollars from the *New York Sun* and a like amount from the *Chicago Daily News*, the *Examiner* now being no longer a market. As the *News* paid only fifty cents, I would send them material that had been rejected by the better markets such as *Life*, which, however, returned everything I sent them during this period. I had an acceptance from *Judge*; they paid fairly well, but upon publication, months away.

To those who would like to ask, How do you write jokes? I can only say, you just write them. Freud and his disciples have attempted to analyze humor (or wit, which is the correct term for these mental acrobatics), but the best book that I have read about it is Max Eastman's fairly recent *The Enjoyment of Laughter*. It may take a special type of brain to originate what are now called "gags"; I don't know. One needs a sense of the ridiculous, plus an excellent memory. This last is needed to prevent the writer from repeating himself, or inadvertently taking old jokes for his own. Some plagiarism used to go on, of course, but I never committed it intentionally, and seldom, I think, by accident. I used to see my jokes reprinted in many places; "The Spice of Life" column in the *Literary Digest* used to have at least one of mine in almost every issue, sometimes credited to British publications such as *Punch* or *The Passing Show*. Newspapers would republish my stuff too, sometimes giving credit to the periodical that had originally bought it, but usually not. The copyright laws fail to protect the jokesmiths, and that is still the case today. Several times I mailed envelopes of jokes, enclosing international reply coupons, to the British humorous magazines with the hope of receiving a few shillings, but I never succeeded in making a sale. Strangely enough, material of more than three or four lines is seldom stolen. Evidently it is considered cricket to pick an author's pants pocket for a dollar, but bad form to put the bee on him for five. A gagman could make a splendid living if he received payment on a royalty basis—if he could receive ten cents, say, each time his handiwork was reprinted, or used on the radio, a few hundred jests might make him financially independent for the rest of his days.

This was before the days of radio, and I've been asked if I'm not sorry for not having stayed in the gag-writing business, as now I might be making a thousand or two thousand dollars a week, which is "what the comedian so-and-so pays his writer." It's a lot of salary, I'll admit, and after paying income tax there should be something left, but I live too close to Hollywood to believe everything I hear about it. It's true that the *top* radio jesters are well paid, and in my opinion they deserve to be. The best of them are not only gag men, but have the ability to originate and develop funny situations. My ambitions were toward fiction. I had already learned that unless the writer of *short* humor develops a style peculiarly his own, as "Bugs" Baer did, for example, he will remain about where he started as far as recognition is concerned.

I believe the greatest humorist of recent times was Ring Lardner, a master of the short-story craft. Like Mark Twain, he was far more than a "funny man." Too much has already been said about the clown whose heart was breaking, but humorists are usually of a melancholy, even morose, case of mind. Mark Twain's life was unhappy, especially his later years, and it is tragic to know that he could lighten the burdens of so many others without easing his own.

In order to withstand the punishment, authors must be the most optimistic of men, and I live upon hope. When I did receive a fair check I would spend it like a sailor on shore leave, feeling certain that there would be a larger one tomorrow—as, of course, there should have been. As a result I was continually in difficulties. Out of the many writers I have met, and known more or less intimately, only one or two had any business sense whatsoever. And why should the world expect them to have any? Is a banker required to write stories?

One Saturday morning, after a particularly lean week, I waited for the postman in front of the decayed mansion where I roomed, and upon collaring him found that the envelopes he had for me were quite uncontaminated with money. There would be no mail delivery in the afternoon, none Sunday, and I had nine cents in cash and stamps.

When I considered that I had no personal belongings to pawn, that my rent and the typewriter hire were due, and that I was already hungrier than a harvester, I decided—and not cheerfully—to apply for a job. I often played pool at the "Y" across the street, when I had the dimes, and chess when I hadn't, and now I interviewed the manager of the Christian Association's employment agency.

CHAPTER 4

For Whom the Bellboy Toils

6. Paul and Nell, ca. 1921. Paul enlisted in the navy while under age. According to his younger brother, George, he stayed just long enough to get a tattoo. *Collection of Patricia Binkley.*

I n my joke-writing days I would never have been guilty of the title that I am giving this chapter. Which shows to what depths a pulp writer can sink.

It was as a hotel bellboy, however, that I went to work. Provided with a note of introduction, I reported that afternoon at one of Denver's largest and swankiest hostelries. Here I was briefly examined by the head bellman, then taken into the basement where I was provided with a locker, a form-fitting, maroon-colored uniform with black silk facings, and a supply of high, white linen collars. I was to work four and twelve hours on alternate days, seven days a week, and was told that while I could expect no salary, my tips would total from thirty dollars a week to more than twice that amount, not at first, perhaps, but after I had learned the ropes. The head bellman even hinted that he could easily charge the boys ten dollars weekly for the privilege of working. But he was too honest for that; he was a square shooter, and if I worked hard, and was a square shooter too, why things would be just dandy.

"You're taking the place of a fellow who wasn't a straight shooter," he said sorrowfully. "I had to dismiss him. Now, you read these printed rules, and I'll explain some special extra rules to you later."

About a dozen bellboys worked on a shift, and most of the "boys" were much older than I; they averaged about twenty-five, and the head bellman, in spite of his rouged cheeks and dyed hair, looked to be forty. One of the bellhops was instructed to take me under his wing for the first day or two and teach me the finer points of the business.

It was the first time I had been in a large hotel, and I was

99

horribly flustered and fearful of doing the wrong thing. The uniform was strange, and the stiff collar wasn't the only uncomfortable thing about it. Feeling like a lonely monkey, I tried to remember what was explained to me, but my mental fog never entirely lifted. The bellhops could use the elevators only when rooming guests, and must use the dark and narrow servants' stairs instead of the grand staircase. There were dozens of other regulations that I can't remember now, nor could I then. We took turns at the various "stations" throughout the lobbies, gradually moving up to the desk where we were given a guest to "room." In charge of his luggage and the keys, we escorted him to his destination on one of the half-dozen floors, and then courteously opened and closed windows and inquired solicitously as to his comfort until he finally came through with the tip. It was almost invariably twenty-five cents, although sometimes a man traveling alone would flip us half a dollar.

When our guest had been taken care of, we would begin again at the farthest station and work toward the desk again, meanwhile running errands for the management—no tips there—or peddling ice water for dimes and quarters, paging, and other duties. To me, a small-town boy, the hotel, with its drugstore, tailor and barbershops, stock exchange, and various dining and ballrooms, was overwhelming. Denver has always gone in for trimmings, and I thought it a shame that H. A. W. Tabor hadn't lived to see this place and its magnificence. He would have loved it. Furthermore, he would have owned it.

I had some little trouble in rooming my first victim. Reaching the elevator with his two suitcases, for the life of me I couldn't remember whether I was to precede him into the car or allow him to step in first. I finally compromised by charging in, with the luggage, at the same time. The wedge was tight and prolonged, but after a scuffle I finally broke it, dropping one suitcase on the foot of my victim, the other across the insteps of the astonished girl operator. When we reached the proper floor, I was again at a loss about the etiquette of who follows whom. Catching my eye, the victim fairly ran from the elevator. I followed, bumping him at every step behind the knees with the two suitcases. In football, this is known as "clipping" and is considered an obnoxious foul.

When we reached his room, he gently but firmly pushed me back out into the hall. I slipped down the back stairs, richer by twenty cents, but with my ears burning.

One day, more than a week later when I should have been thoroughly acquainted with the establishment, I took two commercial travelers to the fourth floor, their key calling for a room in the "annex." The arrangement of the hotel was bewildering at best, and the annex, although newer, was especially so. However, I stepped confidently out of the elevator with my load of bags and briefcases and briskly entered one of the corridors.

"This way, sirs."

Furtively watching the numbers of the rooms we passed, I escorted my charges down toward the end of the long, dimly lit passage, while the much too optimistic traveling men fumbled for change—I could hear their pockets jingling behind me.

Still not finding Room 462, I turned left at the end of the hallway, entering another that looked precisely the same. At the end of this, I again turned left, and oddly passed from the 450s to the 470s.

"Seems like we've walked a mile," one of my charges observed. "Our room's sure a long ways from the elevator."

"I could almost get lost in here," said the other. He wasn't the only one, I thought in desperation. I *was* lost.

"We're almost there," I assured them when, after another turn, they asked questions symptomatic of mental and physical unrest.

We were back in the long row of 450s again. This time I

turned in a new direction, but to my horror, the numbers in the new hallway were in the 90s. There was an unnumbered door at the end of this labyrinth, however, and I advanced upon it hopefully. Putting one bag down, I flung it open. It was a fire escape.

"I'm new here," I remarked brightly.

After making another jog, I set the baggage down through sheer weariness. "Is this the room? Well, it's about time," grunted one of the travelers.

"No. I guess I can't find the room."

"Well, what are we supposed to do? Just stand here?"

"I'll get someone else, sirs," I said, and I strode away with dignity, twice dropping the keys. Once out of view I fled full speed and when I finally found the back stairs, made my way to the lobby where I sought out the head bellman.

"Oh, mercy!" he moaned, wringing his hands, when I told him of my predicament. "Where *are* the guests?"

"They're just standing up there," I said, and my chief snatched the keys with another, shriller "mercy!" and, I suppose, went on a rescue expedition to the fourth floor. If there was a tip, which I doubt, he got it. I expected to be instantly dismissed, but for some reason the affair never reached the ears of management. Nor did I see the two travelers again. Afraid to venture out of the fourth dimension, they may be there yet.

The task most disagreeable to me was paging. When a name was given to me at the desk and I was required to seek out its owner through the lobbies and dining rooms, I was so self-conscious that I could not lift my voice above a whispered mumble.

"Always write the name on a card and put it on one of these silver trays," I was instructed.

"I wouldn't forget the name—at least, I don't think I would."

"That isn't it at all," said my teacher. "The tray is for the tip. I'll show you how it's done."

This bellhop's technique, including the final manipulation of the platter, was perfect, and he had one of the most beautiful paging voices I've ever heard. I tried to imitate his glorious "C—a—w—l fo' Misto' Phillip Chesto' fiel-l-l-ld," but, as in using the telephone, I simply hadn't the gift. Paging continued to cause me acute suffering. Once I was told to page a man who was thought to be attending a meeting of the Metal Miners Association, which was being held in one of the dining rooms—whether it was the Blue Room or the Rainbow Trout Room, I can't remember. At any rate, the speaker was addressing the convention when I entered, and instead of slipping quietly to his desk and handing him the card, I began bawling out "C—a—w—l fo' Misto' so and so," and I kept it up in spite of all the speaker's efforts to continue his speech. Every time I became out of breath he would resume, and then I would cut in again with my plaintive cry, and this went on for a longer time than I now care to think about. I remember that I was finally ushered out of the convention.

It was during this meeting of mine owners, or the one of cattlemen that preceded it, that a huge, fat man shuffled across the marble floor from one of the street entrances. He was ill-dressed and wore a hat of many gallons. I had the "front" station, and when it was whispered to me that this mighty specimen was one of the wealthiest landowners in Colorado, I considered myself in luck. The big fellow insisted upon carrying his own battered, imitation-leather suitcase, but he lumbered after me and I got him roomed without trouble.

As soon as he was inside his moderately priced quarters, he immediately heaved himself onto the bed, muddied boots and all. The mattress sagged about six inches, and when with a pleased grunt he undid his belt and the front of his pants, his stomach rose an equal distance. He closed his eyes, and when he opened them again and saw that I was still arranging the towels and adjusting the window blinds, he frowned and brought out a change purse with many compartments. Beckoning me toward him, he pressed a small, worn dime into my palm.

"This is for you, boy," he signed. "And now I want a woman."

"A what?" I was already backing toward the hall.

"A woman. A blonde-head, if you got one, but I ain't partic'lar." As I continued my shocked silence, he roared: "Keeryst! Ain't you got any wimmen?"

"Not any two-bit ones!" I yelled back as I slammed the door behind me.

When the head bellman became curious and asked me what tip I had received, I told him what had taken place. "Gracious!" he said. "He wanted a woman? Oh, vile." He clacked his tongue, then studied me thoughtfully. "A dime tip. By the way, have you been asked before about—you know."

"Yes. I always get around it by saying I'm new here."

"Good! But hereafter, when they—ask that—you tell me about it right away. Notify me, too, when they ask for—ah—liquor."

"And you'll tell the house detective above it?"

"Well . . . yes. But don't *you* tell him. These things have to be handled with tact."

Of course, I knew that prostitution was carried on in this hotel, even though it was eminently respectable and probably the most conservative in Denver, if not then the most fashionable. The management was surely aware of it. Several very feminine "guests" had cautiously reminded me of their room numbers, if there should be inquiries, but I had taken only an academic interest. Liquor could be bought just around the corner, and there was still a supply of pre-Prohibition St. Louis beer that was sold at fifty cents a bottle. "Leadville sugar moon" was priced at two dollars a pint. I began to understand why the head bellman had wanted to employ a youth from the YMCA. He and the "wise" bellhops made a large profit from bootlegging and pandering, and they wanted nobody horning in on their racket. That explained why all my blunders had been excused; I was a jewel. But I didn't regret the extra money I might have made; my self-respect was taking considerable punishment as things stood, and I knew that the end wasn't far off.

It came one midnight. A guest called downstairs for two bottles of ginger ale and a supply of glasses and ice. On each floor were stations for ice water, but this order had to be carried up from the hotel drugstore. With the glasses shining immaculately on a silver tray, I knocked at the door of a room on the third story, then made a courteous and respectful entrance.

My customer was in the New York cloak and suit business, and was very slightly under the influence of alcohol. The two women in the room reminded me, as far as costume was concerned, of the Denver Academy of Applied Art.

My answer to loud accusations of being late were met with "sorry, sir," for I had learned better than to argue with a guest of the hotel. Then he reviled me for bringing him "feelthy" glasses with my "feenger prints all over them." He was showing off, trying to make evident what a big and resounding shot he was, and I could have endured it if one of his companions hadn't pleadingly interposed in my behalf. When it was over, the gentleman grandly tossed a five-dollar bill on the tray and told me to keep the change. It was five times the largest tip I had yet received, but my gesture was as foolish as his. Leaving it, I stalked out—grandly. The head bellman came into the locker room while I was changing clothes, and without explaining I told him I was quitting.

While working at the hotel I had done little writing, but I still had my typewriter, and I resolved to get busy in good earnest. As an author I might not make half the money as at hopping bells, but at least I could have the pleasant feeling of independence, and there would be no kowtowing or other forms of self-abasement. Like Theodore Roosevelt, I wanted to be able to look any man in the face and tell him to go to hell. (Though, I often wondered, if one is happy and contented with his lot, why tell anyone to go to hell? TR never explained that.)

Several short stories were written during the following weeks; some were submitted to *Black Mask* (now defunct) and others, less hopefully, to *Blue Book* and *Adventure*. These all came back with the customary rejection slips, but in the meantime I had found a new market for jokes: the *American Legion Weekly* (later a monthly) paid a dollar each for several each week. There was a good collection of current newspapers and magazines in the library, and I studied these, sending in batches of fillers everywhere that looked promising. Most papers printed jokes, but unfortunately for me, only a few would pay out good money for originals.

Letters from Father reminded me that writing was a very precarious way of making a living. He suggested journalism, that I might try for a job as a reporter on one of the Denver papers; but instead of taking this good advice, I started a college extension course in pharmacy, which I soon dropped. I also registered at a business school, but never attended any classes. Of all the pursuits, that was the one for which I was probably least fitted.

I couldn't understand what was wrong with my short stories. If it had been the work of someone else, I might have recognized the sophomoric quality of my fiction, but a writer is rather blinded when considering his own brainchildren, especially before he gains experience and develops something of a critical censorship. I expected to have one of my yarns click at any moment—if I could have known what lay ahead of me, I don't know if I would have gone on or not.

"Writing is a trade, and, like any other trade, it must be learned. We must serve our apprenticeship; but we must work it out alone. There are no teachers. We must learn by failure and repeated effort how the thing should be done."[1] Booth Tarkington said it, more than forty years ago, and that opinion can't be improved upon today.

About this time, I wrote a rather naive article that was published in *Writer's Digest*. I called it "Save Your Rejection Slips!" and the idea was that something could be learned from these "writer's cramps," as many magazines made an attempt to outline their needs on the printed form they tucked into returned manuscripts.

The snowy, mile-high winter passed, and one spring evening when I was low in spirits and even lower financially than usual, I thought of some relatives who I had been told were living in Denver. They were very distant ones, and I had never seen them, nor had I heard much about them, but I was homesick and lonely and I looked up their address, which was far out in the northwest side of the city. Lacking carfare, I started my long walk, through downtown Denver and out across one of the smoke-grimed viaducts. I understand that these relatives were old people; and I wondered what kind of welcome I would get.

CHAPTER 5
Darl and Heart

7. Paul wearing chaps, ca. 1923. The chaps are now with his brother George's family. *Author's collection.*

W hen I found the address on the corner of Beech Court, I saw a two-story house of pale yellow brick. Although it was still early, all was dark except for a narrow crack of light at one window. There was a long silence after I had rung the bell on the front porch, but finally something could be heard scampering, like mice, and the shade of the bow window was lifted a few inches, and I saw a small, withered face peering out apprehensively.

"Who is it?" came the quavering little voice. I learned later that it *was* a dreadful time of night; it was almost nine, and my aunt and uncle (the relationship was not really so near) had usually retired by eight thirty. And I was the first visitor they had had in many years.

There was another pause after I had given my name. Then: "You're the doctor's boy? You're Dr. John's boy?" When I assured her that such was the case, I heard the door being unlocked, and I wouldn't have been much surprised if I had heard the rattling of chains as well. I came very near to sprinting off into the darkness.

But she was a nice little old woman. After fastening the door again, she admitted me into the big, dim parlor where we held a pleasant interview, and I could see that she was really glad that I had called. She was very talkative, but spoke for the most part in whispers, and several times put a warning hand to her lips while I was speaking.

"Is someone asleep?" I asked.

She considered for a while, and at last seemed to make up her mind. "I'm going to take you in to see your uncle. He's in bed, but I'm sure you'll be—well—careful. We'll see how you'll affect him."

"Is my—er—uncle ill?"

"Oh, no. He's in good health." She warily led me through the adjoining dining room and into a brightly lit apartment where, stretched out in an enormous bed, lay the long, thin figure of a man, white of hair and mustache.

"Darl," said my aunt breathlessly, "this is Paul Powers—Dr. John's boy."

"Who is it, Heart?"

My aunt repeated the introduction and fully detailed my pedigree, reminding "Darl" of my mother's maiden name and my grandparents on both sides. I picked up his elongated and bony hand, and he let it drop to the counterpane again, saying nothing to me whatever. "It's past your bedtime, Heart" . . . "Yes, Darl, I'm going up now." . . . "Goodnight, Heart." . . . "Goodnight, Darl."

Out in the hall, my aunt lowered her voice again, insisting that I stay overnight. There was an extra bedroom upstairs, across from hers, and tomorrow Darl would be in a better mood. She was very kind, but if I'd had carfare I don't think I would have accepted her hospitality; as it was I remained— for many weeks.

The next morning, in daylight, the house seemed a little less sinister. My aunt was busy in the bright kitchen when I came downstairs, and in an immense case was a large and rather moth-eaten parrot.

"Darl!" it shrieked raucously the moment it saw me, and I jumped backward. When I asked my aunt if the bird belonged to her, she told me that it was Darl's and that it had been with them for nearly thirty years. No, it didn't talk much; if fact, "Darl" was all the creature ever said. The bird shouted the name again, as if in warning that all was not well, and presently Darl himself entered with a peculiar ataxic gait and looked at and past me.

"Heart! Who is this?" He designated me.

Heart told him my name and again outlined the eccentricities of my family tree. Darl made no comment, one way or another, and at breakfast he ate in silence, with a fine appetite, while Heart and I carried on table talk that was, on her part at least, sprightly.

After the meal, Darl lowered his tall form into an easy chair by the window, carefully put on his spectacles, and comfortably unfolded that morning's copy of the *Rocky Mountain News*.

"He's holding it upside down," I cautiously told Heart after following her into the kitchen.

"Darl isn't reading. He's thinking."

Then she asked that I make my home there with them. When I began to make excuses she told me how very lonely she was; self-centered as I was, I was sorry for Heart. It ended with my agreeing to stay, at least for a while. No, she would not listen to my paying anything for my board and lodging; I could do little odd jobs, run errands. My typewriter? Did it make so much noise Darl could hear it downstairs? Then I should bring it. The best time to bring it and my belongings would be in the afternoon. Darl always took a walk in the afternoons when the weather was fine.

"But if uncle objects to me . . ."

"Darl will get used to you."

Darl never did. Each morning with great surprise he would ask who I was, why I was there, and how long I intended to stay. When I tried to help with the furnace in the morning—the house was kept like an oven—he would follow me and the ash can up the basement steps, muttering imprecations and whisking up my footprints. Once at mealtime he sat watching me intently, mumbling "twenty-one, twenty-two, twenty-three . . ." He was counting my mouthfuls. When Heart reproved him for it he hid a slow grin behind his napkin. Darl wasn't so crazy! He wasn't pleased at my presence there, and he was clever at showing how he felt about it. Usually he ignored me completely, and spent hours whispering to the parrot. The bird would squawk "Darl!" and stare at me with malevolence, making an effort to spear me with its beak whenever I came close to its cage. Darl and Heart were accustomed to only two meals daily, and for lunch I contented myself with a bottle of milk smuggled in from the corner grocery.

Darl was always immaculate, and in the afternoons he would stalk out in all his finery, swinging a walking stick, and with his snowy mustache and aristocratic face, looking very distinguished indeed. He never spoke to anyone on these walks.

There was a large Edison phonograph in the parlor. I hadn't dared suggest putting it in operation, but one day Heart breathlessly suggested that I put on one of the heavy, stove-lid records. Darl had just gone out.

"I want to hear it; I've been wanting to hear it for a long time," she whispered. "I'll watch at the window. Maybe you can play it three or four times before he comes back."

We did play three or four records, feeling like partners in crime. That day Heart told me of a "tantrum" in which Darl had aroused her in the middle of the night and ordered her to slide down the banister.

"I was in my nightdress. It was terrible," Heart said, awed at the memory.

"What did you do?"

"I slid down the banister."

I remained with Darl and Heart for some weeks, but finally I weakened. Heart had been made happy by my coming, and now I caused Darl great pleasure by my departure. He actually grasped my hand at the door and beamed at me. "And so you're Dr. John's boy! Well, well! It's too bad you can't visit us for awhile."

Still homesick, but reluctant to return to Kansas, I boarded the little narrow-gauge train that climbed in those days through Golden and on up to Black Hawk. The railroad had once ascended several more steep, switchback miles to Central City, but that portion of the track had been abandoned during the First World War. Some of my earliest childhood memories were of Black Hawk and Central, for I had spent summer vacations here, even attended fourth grade one winter in the ancient frame schoolhouse. Here lived relatives of mine—near ones. The mining district had produced a great amount of gold and silver since 1859, but was a ghost camp now, with great ore dumps scarring the naked hills and decaying mine buildings everywhere. Its long history made the place all the more fascinating to me, for it was here, when it was known as the Greggory Diggings, that the first real mining of Colorado gold began. My early exposure to Black Hawk's atmosphere had given me the ambition to someday write about it.

My cousin Elsie had written a song. Unfortunately, as so many others had done, and still do, she had fallen prey to a music "publisher." This buzzard had persuaded the girl to pay a "fee" of about one hundred dollars, after making her many smooth promises (all so cleverly worded that he violated no law), and in return he had "published" the song. What she had to show for the family's hard-gathered money was a stack of cheap and messily printed sheets with, I think, even her name misspelled on the flimsy covers. Not understanding the cruel hoax that had been played upon her, she still had hope. . . . Elsie had been practically blind since her babyhood, and shortly after this her darkness became total forever.

Many years later I was to be thrilled at hearing Mrs. Roosevelt announce the name of this talented woman as the winner of high honors in a contest for blind writers.

This "Get Wealthy as a Song Writer" racketeer infuriated me at the time, and I have done my best to fight the scoundrels ever since. They have been exposed many times, and vigorously, but they are still with us, merely varying their methods. I wonder who first thought of this lucrative business of rooking would-be writers, anyhow. How many millions they must gather each year from the inexperienced! Why doesn't Congress, or somebody, pass a—I won't say it; I'm tired of saying it.

While I was in Black Hawk a new feature began to appear in large-city newspapers throughout the country. It was a double column of short humorous material: a cartoon, a witty verse or two, and half a dozen two-line jokes. It was carried by one of the best-known syndicates, and called *The Laugh Factory*, or that is near enough. I will disguise it here, as well as the name of *The Laugh Factory*'s editor, whom I will call Harold Claymore Montague. Anyhow, I sent a batch of jokes to one of the papers carrying the column, and after several weeks I received a check for the best items and a letter from Montague in New York asking me to submit more. I was greatly cheered, as this gave indications of being another regular market with a weekly remittance. If I could sell consistently to *The Laugh Factory*, the *Chicago Daily News*, and the *American Legion Weekly*, and get an acceptance now and again from other publications, I would practically be on easy street.

So I got married and brought a wife with me back to Kansas.

CHAPTER 6

Ad Astra Per Aspera,
Add Aspirin

8. Paul and baby Jack, 1925. Paul was just beginning his pulp-writing career at this point. *Author's collection.*

As every Kansas schoolboy knows, the first four words of this chapter heading are the motto of his state and, translated, mean: "To the stars through difficulties." I was to learn that a callow youth of just turned nineteen who expects to establish and support a family by his writings will see plenty of stars, whether he ever reaches them or not. But as Conrad said, and H. L. Mencken has said more recently: "Ah, Youth . . ."

When Father recovered from his surprise, and the disappointment he tried not to make too evident, he advanced me the few hundred dollars from my mother's insurance policy, which I was supposed to receive when I reached twenty-one. Aided by this, I rented a cottage, bought some furniture, which included a "new" rebuilt typewriter from Chicago, and with great optimism set up housekeeping. The townspeople view me with suspicion. I had no honest means of support that they could see. I was looked upon as downright lazy, and peculiar as well. I never "worked." Probably my father supported me in secret. This attitude on the part of the community (and this distrust if not actual dislike extended to my wife, as well) might have made me a paranoiac in short order had I been a little more sensitive. And I was sensitive enough. In varying degrees I have been confronted with this attitude wherever I went, and there is even a little of it in such writer colonies as Laguna Beach and Santa Fe. Even now, when a strange barber asks me my business, I usually lie to him. A writer wants to be considered human—and even normal—like anyone else.

As far as my work was concerned, things seemed encouraging. I sent a packet of jokes several times a week to Mr. Montague of *The Laugh Factory*, and he would select a joke or two from each. He began to write me letters, too, and I received one every few days. I had never before had personal correspondence with a real editor, and I was flattered and stimulated. At about this time *Life* raised its price for jokes to five dollars each, and if I remember rightly, the first one I sold at this new figure was this one:

Lawyer: Have you any assets?
Client: Well, I've entered a prize contest.

In the mid-1920s, when contests were beginning to get in stride, that might have been considered mildly funny; I don't know. But this joke really symbolized my own outlook.

Try as I would, I couldn't sell consistently to *Life* at this period; the envelopes would usually come back with the little green-and-yellow slips enclosed, but when I did land something I was much elated. The old *Life* was tops in humor at that time; *Puck* was dead, and although *Judge* was still much in evidence, only London's *Punch* ranked with *Life*, which was now edited by Mr. Robert E. Sherwood, with Mr. Robert Benchley as dramatic critic. I sold epigrams as well as jokes now and then, also for five dollars, and as some of them ran less than ten words, I was pleased to be able to say that my word rate was higher than Rudyard Kipling's, then the highest-paid writer in the world.

But we were soon in financial difficulties for all that, and in a few months I was at, and below, bedrock, and with bills outstanding, small but accumulating. Sometimes I would write sixty or more jokes a day, jotting down the central ideas on an old envelope and typing them out in final form later, but of course most of these were duds. When they had been the rounds, and the fifty-cents-paying *Chicago Daily News* had rejected them too, I threw them away. If I had concentrated every effort on these "squibs," as the editor of the local paper called them, we might have done better at this time, but I was ambitious. I wanted to write fiction. *Action Stories* had me on nerves' edge for a couple of weeks, when J. B. Kelly, then the editor, wrote a brief note saying that they were holding a yarn for "further consideration," but it finally came back again with no "further" explanation. The story—I never did sell it—dealt with imaginary exploration in Central Asia, about which I knew almost nothing. I was trying every sort of fiction that year, aiming at everything from the *Saturday Evening Post* on down. Later, when I heard that the novel *Main Street* had been rejected by the *Post* and returned to Mr. Lewis, I lost some of my respect for this magazine.

Most of my efforts were concentrated on the string of magazines published by Street & Smith. This company, which had brought out Nick Carter and Frank Merriwell, was probably the oldest of all pulp publishers.[1] I sent manuscripts to each of their many weekly and monthly publications, and kept sending them. Their rejection slips, on which their tall, gloomy New York building was reproduced, became very familiar and distasteful to me. Most of my work went to their *Western Story*, which, being a weekly, used a large amount of material. But none of mine. I now know something of the reason for these rejections. The ideas were usually all right; the fact that I could sell jokes was proof that I had some gift of originality. But the technique of fiction writing, even pulp fiction as a matter of fact, isn't picked up overnight. This technique, or sense of form, is something that grows gradually. None of the writer's textbooks that I have read can furnish any shortcuts, although they seem correct enough in theory, and certainly have much to say about such things as "coherence" and "emphasis" and other confusions that can be found in any freshman book on English composition. Some of the more recent books on "How to Write Short Stories" try a different approach, but the old trial-and-error method of collecting rejection slips is still the best.

Before I had been married a year I found myself a father, and then more than ever it grew upon me that writing jokes for a living was no joke. Most writers do their best under a little pressure, and I am no exception to the rule, but too much pressure is something else again. It's hard to be funny, or even rational, when the wolf has his head inside. An author can function with food, perhaps, but if he's worried and without coffee or tobacco, he's tempted to say to hell with it and go out and get a job.

It's easy to overdramatize these sufferings, which were, of course, mostly mental, but they were real enough. In some of his short stories, James Stephens, author of *The Crock of Gold*, has pictured this kind of despair; he has written of it more effectively than any other writer I know. But his frustrated characters were jobless, and I had work, and did work at almost every waking hour. Young writers have asked me why it is that a beginning writer can't be paid *something*, if only a very little, for the fruits of his toil, as the apprentices in other trades earn while they learn. If there's an answer to that, I don't know what it is, but I usually reply, comfortingly, that he is lucky not to be compelled to lay out from seven to twelve thousand dollars for the opportunity to learn his chosen profession, as every doctor of medicine must. All *he* needs is a typewriter, the ability that God gave him, and that all-important intestinal ingredient. But unless he's cleverer than most of us, he'll know he's been in a fight.

And, if he's *really* got viscera, and if he's not content to write merely for the money that's in it, the fight will get tougher as he goes on.

One of the local grocers cut off my credit that winter, my account having reached the horrifying total of nineteen dollars, and after store hours he would haunt the streets I had to traverse on my way to and from the post office. Or so it seemed to be then. It was horribly humiliating, as were other happenings. When we were out of coal and my wife went to the dealer to order more, he refused to deliver any until I had paid for the last ton. "He sends you in here to ask for credit— why doesn't he come in himself?" the man asked her with a knowing smile. I was infuriated, naturally. The community, a sizable part of which owed my father for his services, and had nothing against the convenience of credit as such, was having its little revenge on her; it was "taking me down a peg or two." I was being persecuted a little, for the good of my soul. It was believed that, for wanting to be a writer, I thought I was "smart." If they could only have known how humble I was, in the presence of my typewriter . . .

I had ordered a new heating stove from a Kansas City mail-order company, five dollars down and five a month, and I unwrapped the thing with a great deal of pride and with much admiration of its nickelwork and isinglass doors. Having no fuel, I burned the crate and the wrappings it came in. Then I fed it old jokes—until it roared. When a real cold snap came I managed to overcome the temptation of dark nights and the coal pile of my neighbor, old Mr. Eaton; and I made the discovery that bits of coal could be picked up on the alleys—when no one was looking. I took my typewriter into the kitchen and worked by the kerosene stove until monoxide poisoning nearly overcame me. Sometimes I wouldn't have much cared if it had.

My father would, and did, cheerfully help me out, but with the arrogance of a twenty-year-old, I hated to take assistance, even from him. There was a salt mine at the edge of town, and I asked for and obtained work there, hoping to work after hours and on Sunday at the writing machine.

I had worked briefly at the plant before, during a summer school vacation, though usually I had preferred farm work, shucking wheat at harvest time. This mine was about seven hundred feet deep, and the diggings were old and extensive, the salt being taken out to leave enormous rooms supported by great salt pillars. A weak strength of dynamite was used in blasting, and the drills were electrically powered. The miners were mostly Mexicans and were paid according to the number of cars they were able to break up and load onto the cages. One giant Sonoran was said to draw as high as eight dollars a day, and if so, he earned his money, for the plant was owned by a Chicago packing concern that was delighted at the low Kansas labor costs and took every advantage of the state's reactionary, farmer-dominated viewpoint on all labor questions.

I worked topside, in the loading gang. We worked ten hours at thirty-five cents an hour, and no extra for overtime, and this was when the country was at the height of its so-called prosperity, with Wall Street shares on the way to their fantastic top that blew off four years later. It was hard work, but I was husky, and the worst part of it for me was the monotony and the mental emptiness that went with the job. The ten hours passed with the horrible slowness of a marijuana dream, and I came home too tired to do much writing, though my mind certainly should have been rested. The great chunks of salt brought up from below were dropped in at the top of the tipple house, and after being broken up into different sizes in the mill, the salt was poured into huge bins. Although almost pure, none of it was used as table salt—practically all of it went to the meatpackers.

Empty railroad cars had to be "pinched" with hand bars from the siding onto the scales, and here they were loaded to capacity with salt of a certain grade number, the coarseness ranging from that of fine sand to lumps the size of large marbles. A man or two had to climb into one of the vast bins, up in the bowels of the tipple house, and keep the salt running through the chutes while others worked in the cars. In winter the bins were like iceboxes, and in the summer they were stifling. About half the orders were for sacked salt, and these sacks, weighing two hundred pounds each, were hand-trucked into the freight cars, stood in tiers, and other sacks thrown on top of these, this requiring a certain amount of muscle. One young Mexican became so dexterous in sewing up the sacks that the big boss, the superintendent of the plant, once stood admiring his cleverness for upwards of half an hour. He gave the boy a cigar—the first and only bonus every granted by the company. But then, the boss's salary was not large either; he was a Scotchman and the cigar was no small gift.

Working with us was a thin and undernourished war veteran of about thirty, and how this little man, with his chronic cough and blue lips and fingers, ever endured the hard labor was something I never understood. No doubt the wife and five small children who lived in one of the horrible little company houses gave him his inspiration, but at any rate he was the most cheerful and optimistic of us all. A few years later he died, probably from gout.

The company had the quaint habit of driving us hard for four or five days, then laying us off without pay. Another queer thing it did was to pump saltwater into an apple orchard a quarter of a mile away, and they continued to do this until every tree had been killed. The orchard was owned by my father. He never did anything about it except protest mildly to Superintendent Dowie once or twice. Father hated litigation; and besides, Mr. Dowie was a friend of his.

I went to Newton, a railroad division point east of us, and applied for a job as brakeman. I was desperately near scrapping my writing ambitions. Accepted, I was told to report back when called, which would be in a week or two.

Then a thin letter came in the mail and hallelujah! I had sold a sure-enough short story to a nationally circulated magazine. Farnsworth Wright, the editor of *Weird Tales*, informed me that "The Death Cure" had been accepted and that I would be paid at the rate of one-half cent a word, $21.75. I ran around the house like a man demented, and wound up at Father's with the news. I was congratulated, but with some reserve. Everyone seemed able to hold their emotions pretty much in check.

But to me this seemed a marvelously good omen, and I remembered having read that just such a thing had happened to Jack London, except that he was ready to take a job as a postman when a magazine acceptance caused him to change his plans. I wouldn't have to take the brakeman job on the Santa Fe! And on the strength of these new hopes I quit work at the salt plant.

I immediately wrote other stories for Mr. Wright, and several were accepted in the space of a few weeks. Unfortunately, there was that strange "pay on publication" fly in the ointment. I have a little notebook before me in which I kept the records of those days, and I find that it was eight months almost to the day before I was paid the $21.75 for that first story. The checks for the others were equally belated. Of course, this is an unfair practice. *Weird Tales* may have changed their policy since (they did offer me three-quarters of a cent a word two years later, which I felt able to decline), but at this time, at any rate, they were what could be called a Class C market. But I remain very thankful for those acceptances, for they came at a time when I needed encouragement. And I liked the magazine. Some very good work was being published in it; my mind ran, at times, toward the pseudoscientific, and especially toward the horror tale. I was then, and am still, a great admirer of H. G. Wells's earlier work along this line, and I think he will be remembered, in the long run, for those highly imaginative stories rather than his heavier sociological studies—he wouldn't like it that way, but posterity, too, will much rather be amused than bored. In one issue of *Weird Tales* Mr. Wells had a story adjoining one of mine, and I wondered how much *he* was paid for the American serial rights.

There was another insect in this magazine's salve. When it bought a story, it bought *all* rights—not just the first serial, which many publications are content with. In order that there might be no mistake, a rubber stamp on the back of the check claimed that the endorser had sold "book rights, dramatic rights, first and second serial rights, motion picture rights, foreign publication rights." In fact, the story was the author's no longer, and as far as that story went, he had sold himself out of house and home. Nowadays, of course, radio rights (big networks, little networks, foreign networks and independent broadcasting stations, all wireless rights domestic and foreign, with and without television) would be included in what the writer is asked to sign away.

Just for an example, here's how it worked out in my case. Among the stories of mine that were published in *Weird Tales* were "The Life Serum" and "Monsters of the Pit," the latter being featured on the cover. I received about fifty dollars for the two (not for each) and some ten years elapsed. I had forgotten the yarns until one day I happened to open the current *Best Short Stories of 1929*—by O'Brien. This annual volume contained a list of short stories that had been published in book form during the twelvemonth. I was surprised to see my name there as the author of "Monsters of the Pit" and "The Life Serum," which had just been published in a collection edited by Herbert Asbury: *Not at Night.* It was the first I'd heard about it, and I ordered a copy. When it came, I found the "blurb" on the dust jacket extremely interesting. It stated that the book had been published in England under a different title and that it had sold more than 100,000 copies there. As only a few authors were represented, and I had two stories in the volume, I estimated that my share of the royalties should have been several thousand dollars, not including those from the American publication of the book. Of course, there was nothing I could do, except smile—with my teeth in close contact. Somebody must have made considerable money out of the work that I had done on a rather empty stomach ten years before—but they made it legally. If I had received some complimentary copies of the book I might not have felt so indignant.

The beginning writer must keep his eye out—and remember that some publishers will not only try to get his work for next to nothing, but will cheerfully act as his agent for the rest of his days, their fee being 100 percent of the proceeds.

Stimulated by one magazine's acceptances, I resumed my attack on the others. I even wrote and sold a "confession" story in which I was an innocent and deceived girl unused to the city and its wicked ways; but although I received an immediate check at a good rate, my artistic conscience, if any, was hurt a little, and I didn't follow up this then good-paying field. My story wasn't immoral, or even very suggestive. But it was nauseous tripe, and though I did try another or two, I couldn't get my "heart" into it, and I put all thought of these markets out of mind.

Action Stories bought a brief tale of mine about this time for thirty dollars, but the longer yarns I sent them immediately afterward all bad-pennied home.

Some ten years earlier, I remember, I had peddled some papers in our town, lurid sheets titled the *Saturday Blade* and *Chicago Ledger*, the last being the sensational magazine section of the weekly paper. I didn't sell very many. One day "down at the train" a man with a nickel in his hand had leaned out of the smoker and called "Hey, Boy!" I had rushed toward him filled with elation, but was plunged into the depths of humiliation when the traveler curled his nose and said: "I don't want one of those damn things; give me a *Saturday Evening Post.*" I'll never forget the smile of the town's nice boy, who stood next to me with his neat bag of *SEPs*. Now I sent the *Ledger* some fiction—not forgetting the old incident—and my earlier sufferings were rewarded with acceptance. When I saw the checks, however, I was humiliated again. They were for eight and ten dollars; a rate of a quarter of a cent a word. Discouraged, I returned to my joke writing.

I seemed to be making considerable headway with the syndicate. Soon I was writing practically all the short humor in *The Laugh Factory* and was receiving an almost daily letter from Harold Claymore Montague. He believed in keeping in close touch. The *Factory* was signed with his name at the top, and I rather resented the fact that only a small part of my material was given my byline. Worse, an occasional bright bit of mine was initialed H.C.M. A writer's future depends to a large degree in his success at making his name known to the public, and I spent a considerable part of my time being a little mad at Mr. Montague. The artist who furnished the daily cartoon was careful to sign his moniker in plain letters. It was Carl Anderson, whose "Henry," the little boy with the hydrocephalic skull, was later to bring him fame and, I hope, fortune.

At Christmas, Mr. Montague had sent us a gift. It came at a time when we were especially poor, and we opened the large box with a great deal of expectancy. It contained a gallon-sized barrel of green glass and sterling silver, equipped with faucet and drinking cups. It was overwhelming. And empty.

"Well?"

"Sure swell, isn't it?"

"But—could we sell it?" my wife mused.

"Not in this town we couldn't," I said regretfully. "We'd better not even show it."

A little later Mr. Montague thrilled me by sending a contract for me to sign. At last, the word "Contract" was typed at the top of the document. I had always imagined that in a contract promises were made by *both* parties, but when I signed this I agreed to send *The Laugh Factory* all the humorous material I wrote during the year "before submitting it for publication elsewhere." This meant that Mr. Montague would have first look, and that markets paying more money, such as *Life*, would have only his rejections to consider. I was promised nothing in return, not even that a certain number of jokes would be accepted by him each week. I signed it, not knowing what else to do, and regretted it later. In all justice to Mr. Montague, however, he did send me regular checks, at times adding an "advance" to keep it at a reasonable figure. I was soon owing him work.

CHAPTER 7

A Novel, and What Didn't Come of It

9. Four generations of the Powers family, 1925. *From left:* Paul, holding baby Jack; Paul's grandmother Susannah Powers; and Paul's father, John Harold Powers. By this time, John Powers's patience had been significantly tested by Paul's nonconformist lifestyle. Paul's 1949 novel *Doc Dillahay* was loosely based on his father's life, and he gave Susannah's maiden name, Dillehay, to the central character, John Dillahay. *Author's collection.*

B rashly, I "elected" myself to the Kansas Authors' Club that spring. I was only to belong to the organization for a year, for although the dues were small the society had nothing for me. The great majority of the listed members weren't writers at all, not to my way of thinking. With a few notable exceptions they were members of women's clubs who had written something or other, and who imagined themselves to be authors. I met one or two, and I grew to think of the group as "The Mutual Admiration Society." To one who had to write for a living, with no time for posing, the club had little to offer. I hope it has improved since. The only organization that would be of real help to a beginning writer would be one such as the Author's League of America. Unfortunately for the tyro who isn't yet selling his work, its membership is open only to genuine professionals with an income mainly derived from authorship.

The writers' magazines carried many advertisements of typists, agents, and other services, and I now decided to earn extra money by hanging out my shingle as a critic. My ignorance included not knowing how ignorant I was. I had only three or four books, one of them a dictionary; there was still no library in the town, and the only fairly recent encyclopedia (not the *Britannica*) was at the high school. Still, I had been selling some fiction, not much, but some, and I had learned considerable in the last two years. I inserted a small advertisement in the *Writer's Digest*, offering to pass judgment upon manuscripts for the modest fee of seventy-five cents per thousand words, and announced that my specialty was Westerns and adventure stories.

The response was fairly good, but I never renewed the ad. During the month or two that followed I learned something of what an editor is up against. And something more, too, about human nature, and writers' nature in particular. Wanting to make up in hard work and sincerity what I lacked in experience, I carefully studied the scripts that were sent to me and wrote very honest opinions, sometimes at great length (some of my criticisms were nearly as long as the stories criticized). I soon came to the conclusion, however, that the authors of the manuscripts didn't really want unbiased analysis, even of the most constructive kind; they wanted praise, and lots of it. Or, it would be kinder to say, they were so hungry for encouragement that they would pay out good money to get it. I should have understood that, for I was starved for it myself. Nowadays I pass on reviewing a manuscript if I possibly can; not only is my judgment very fallible, but it's a hard chore, and nearly always a thankless one. Writers simply don't like to be told of the brainchild's faults. When they say they do, they lie. I am infuriated myself when an editor points out defects in my work, even when my good sense tells me that he is right. Not for nothing are critics despised people!

From Seattle came an express package containing an enormous book manuscript. It had been typed by some "agency," probably at great expense, on sheets of paper 13 inches long instead of the 8½ x 11 size that editors insist upon. With it came a letter badly misspelled in pencil:

Dear Mr. Powers,

I havenent got any monny to send with this but if it is eny good sell it and I will go share and share alike. I am an old sailer shipped befoar the mast when I was forteen yrs. of age. I am now a shoemaker 76 yrs. of age. You can see by reading the story of my life I have ben around the horn eight times in windjammers and have seen most of the World. Hopping to year from you, I remane,

Yrs. Truely.

Thrilled at the prospect of discovering another Dana or a Melville, I went to work on the manuscript. But it was terrible. The accursed agency had obviously revised it in an attempt to make it "literary," and of course for the worse. In spite of the added trouble it would have involved, I would rather have had it as its author had originally scrawled it out. Even then, it would have been hopeless. It was simply a tiresome account of one voyage after another, and the only color in it were the glamorous (in the 1920s) names of Hong Kong, Bombay, Calcutta, Yokohoma, and the other exotic ports visited. Such manuscripts usually contain too much stilted descriptive matter; this one contained none at all. "We unloaded cargo at Callao and sailed down the cost of Chile to Antofagasta where we took on a cargo of nitrates, then we sailed for the Straits of Magellan." Nothing ever seemed to happen, although of course plenty did. When a man was washed overboard, he was simply overboard, and "his name was Johnson and he was 23 years of age." The author was very careful of dates, and he accurately gave the names of the captains and mates, but the story as well as the ships seemed always in the doldrums. If it is possible for a deep-sea yarn to be as dry as dust, this one was. And yet how much life the old shoemaker must have seen during his four or five decades on sailing ships! How was it possible to set down more than a hundred thousand words without writing just one interesting paragraph? If he had encountered Moby Dick, he might have written: "Saw a white whale today with lots of old rusty harpoons sticking in it; whale also had a ship's longboat in its mouth which was filled with seamen. Weather clean, wind south by east." I wrote the old gentlemen a letter, telling him how I felt about his book, praising what I could find to praise, which was not much, and explaining why I thought it would be a waste of postage to submit it to publishers. He owed me nothing, I assured him, but what should I do with the book? In his gloomy reply, he told me that he had already spent a lot of money on the manuscript, and that he guessed it was no good and to burn it. I kept it for several months, but upon moving to another house I did destroy the book. And within a week I received word from its author requesting that I send it back.

My best customer was a woman living in a distant part of Kansas. She sent me four or five scripts altogether, each accompanied by a draft for three or four dollars signed by her banker husband. There was something chilly about those signatures, and I sweated and did my best to make criticisms worth the money. My client did have some talent, and I could encourage her a little without disturbing my conscience too much. However, one day a script arrived that seemed much below her average. It was titled "In Lieu of Trousers." After reading the story, I lambasted it unmercifully, and I remember that I was especially severe in dealing with the first paragraphs. It was supposed to be a humorous story, and I told the banker's wife that even the title was unpleasantly fragrant, that the French word "lieu" should be taboo, and that "Instead of Trousers" would be far better, or, if she wanted to get really down to the seat of things: "Instead of Pants."

I heard no more from her, and later on I discovered that "In Lieu of Trousers" was an unfinished story by Mark Twain and that she had "finished" it. I don't believe she did it to trap me; she was trying for a contest of some kind. At any rate, I was greatly chagrined, though I tried not to think too much about it.

"And so you," somebody accused me, "*you* criticized Mark Twain!"

"Well, who is Mark Twain that he should be above criticism?" I retorted, and if Mark Twain really did write the beginning of that awful thing, which I sometimes doubt, he deserved what I handed him. He did write some fearfully unfunny things in his time, and along with his masterpieces were some awful duds.

I gave up commenting on the manuscripts of others and began to give all my attention to my own. They stood in need of it. Over a space of several months I sold only one, a "short short" to *Real Detective Tales and Mystery Stories*. The yarn was one of my worst, I thought even at the time, but curiously enough I saw it given honorable mention, much later, in the annual "O. Henry Memorial Award Prize Stories." I still wonder what was the matter with the editor the day she selected it. Well, it only goes to show . . .

I wanted to emulate the late F. Scott Fitzgerald and be a famous novelist before I was old enough to vote. A modest ambition, surely. Fitzgerald was then at the height of his popularity, and was as imitated by young writers as Hemingway was to be in later years, though Fitzgerald's influence was in the long run neither deep nor lasting. I wasn't a great admirer of his work, but I did envy his success. The mood in which I formulated my ideas for a novel, I am now humbly aware, was unworthy. I was silly and conceited—not that conceited and silly men haven't written books. But I wasn't ready for a novel; I was years short of being ready.

I went ahead anyhow. What I was going to offer was just a long story, long enough to be put within book covers, not real life or even my conception of what real life was. I had read Harry Leon Wilson's *Merton of the Movies*, and without Mr. Wilson's skill (I imagined I had his humor), I planned a story of an unsophisticated hero. He wasn't, by far, as unsophisticated as I was. He was named, I think, Dale Apple, just a small-town young man with great ambition.

The first thing I learned was that it is much easier to dream of writing a book than to write it; setting it down on paper took hard work, and months of it. I found that to get it done, I had to neglect the meal ticket I had with *The Laugh Factory* and the other buyers of my humorous bits. I found myself unable to do two entirely different kinds of creative work at the same time. Although my book was to have its humorous spots, I fondly hoped, still it had an undercurrent of seriousness, and I wanted to give everything to it until it was finished. When I was well into it, I was stuck with it. Joke writing went by the board.

I took up work again at the salt plant, much against my will. It wasn't a long session, but it served to increase my natural dislike of backbreaking labor. I wouldn't have liked it at its rate of pay, even if there had been nothing to do.

The biggest moneymaker among the salt miners was Ned Luff. He was said to have suffered a brain injury in childhood—he certainly couldn't have received one afterward. When I first knew him he unloaded railroad cars of coal in the big, red-painted chute where we boys used to play sometimes, and he was always black with its dust. Later, when someone persuaded him that he could make more money at the plant, he went to work there, changing in color from black to gray, and finally, when the salt had deposited a thick enough layer, to white. The management was delighted with Ned, as he had no sense of fatigue as normal persons had after exertion. He was only of average build, but the amount of work he did was amazing. I have forgotten his record number of cars of salt loaded in one day—I'm afraid it would be unbelievable if I set it down here—it was nearly twice that of the runner-up, the Mexican giant. Ned worked with the fury of a man demented, which of course he was.

He had a lot of money to spend, as he was paid by the number of tons of salt mined. Once I saw him pull out a double handful of gold watch chains. He didn't brave the mysteries of owning a watch, however. Another time when I met him on the street he stopped me and displayed a large board, on which hundreds of dice of various colors and sizes had been glued.

"What's it for, Ned?" I asked, not pretending my amazement. He was a jovial fellow, but I always stood poised ready to run, just in case.

"Oh, I tunno tid. But ain't it pretty? T'ese tices *here*," he said, pointing out a pair in one corner, "t'ese tice is *loated*—tost me fi' tollars, tid."

I lost track of Ned, and don't know how long his body lasted, but he was, as I said, making good wages, and he found someone—or rather, someone found him—willing to go through a ceremony of holy matrimony. Unlike many of his mental status, he had known nothing whatever about sexual relations, and if he had heard things relating to it he considered it all a joke. It was all amazingly new to him.

"Well, Ned, how's married life?" I asked him not long afterward.

He gave me a punch in the ribs that nearly knocked me down, grinning the while. "I'll tell you all about it, tid," and I wish I could put down, as he gave it, his details of the mechanics of the business. I don't know if Ned ever raised a family of "tids," but I fervently hope not.

When we changed to another rented house, we found ourselves next door to the one occupied by Rufe Strunkman, his wife, and seven children ranging in age from an infant to one of about twelve. Rufe, who was past fifty, was a salt plant worker in poor health, a taciturn man who shuffled to and from the job in shoes that had been cut with a knife to make room for his dropsical ankles. I was talking with my father on the street one day when Rufe came up, dinner pail in hand, on his way home.

"Keep your pants on, Doc," he said.

I laughed after he had shuffled off. "What did he mean by that?" I asked.

"He wants me to be ready for a night call—they're expecting another baby," Father said without enthusiasm. "By the look of Rufe himself, I'm afraid I'm going to be called for something else."

He was, in the daytime. Rufe died after being off work less than a week, and a great yell of woe that we could hear inside our house announced the fact. A little later we saw at least five of the children outside the fatal bedroom, peering through the screen of the open window with their hands cupped about their eyes. The smaller ones brought boxes to stand on. The oldest boy saw me on the porch, and shouted, with a grin that showed the notches of his Hutchinson's teeth: "Papa's dead in there! He died! Papa died!"

These and similar horrors decided me that I *would* escape, that I would use what brains the gods had given me and become a writer. I felt pity for those unable to escape—who didn't try. Although there is nothing degrading in unskilled labor, I thought, and still do think, that there is plenty of room for improvement in the laborer's standard of living and dying. What could I do, I wondered, to help them out? Well, I could lighten the troubles of some of them, perhaps, by giving them entertainment. The pulp magazines filled a need, for these people didn't buy books.

But I continued to work on my novel, even though I, who was fathering it, doubted this brainchild at times. A novel that one has to "plot" isn't my present idea of a novel, and instead of being based on observations of life, this one grew out of a certain superficial cleverness that my amateurish technique did not improve. Instead of laughing at my hero, I should have laughed at myself.

One scorching August day, while I was finishing the last chapter, the news swept through the neighborhood that the postmaster of our town had been found hanging from a tree in a gully half a mile away, a suicide. Ray had been well liked in the town; he was a war veteran not long married, a big, powerfully muscled fellow, and the last person you would have suspected of a mental distress so overwhelming. As I trotted toward the scene of the tragedy—half the town ran there too—the grotesque thought came to me that maybe I had something to do with it. Certainly I had caused Ray more trouble than any other "customer," with my "postage-dues," the weighings of manuscripts, and my continual yammering of "Is the mail distributed yet, Ray?" And now Ray wouldn't have the privilege of "weighing in" my most stupendous script, the novel. Not a comfortable thought—maybe he had heard that I was writing one!

When I reached the ravine the cut-down body still lay on the ground, the discolored arms folded, the blued face partially covered with a handkerchief. A writer should have been more interested in the awed crowd that had gathered than in the thing it was staring at—it was strange, I remember, the different ways in which people were affected by the happening. I walked home a good deal more slowly than I had come. In spite of the fierce sun, I felt chilled. It had seemed to me that a horrible, nameless something had leaped about and gibbered and made obscene gestures among the branches of the tree. How little I knew of the human heart! In the hardware store where Ray had bought the rope, he had been jokingly asked: "What are you going to do, Ray? Hang yourself?" And he had answered, "Sure." If only some of his friends could have known beforehand of his despondency—but then I've learned since that there is no way for a man to tell his troubles, no way for others to understand if he did; even though everyone says, after such a tragedy: "Why didn't he let us know?" Suppose he had? Before a sufferer is really listened to, he has to prove his case in the way Ray did, which makes it rather too late all around. Anyhow, thinking of all this, I had a rather poorer opinion of the book I was writing.

I did finish it that night, but not with the burst of enthusiasm I had anticipated.

A postal inspector weighed the script for me the next day—there had been nothing wrong with Ray's accounts, though that is always the first thing people think of—and then began a period of nervous waiting. Would the book be accepted? I had sent it to one of the most prominent of New York publishers. Well, to make the story of a bad story short, some five weeks later a small envelope was pushed into my post office box, a thin one bearing the publisher's name in the upper left-hand corner. I opened it, somehow, with my pulses racing, for didn't a letter mean acceptance?

The letter briefly informed me that my book manuscript was "not available" and that it was being returned under separate cover.

I often wondered what publishers mean by the phrase "not available." The story is always available if a writer submits it to them and it's in their hands. Of course it's available. They don't want it, that's all, and why don't they say so?

When I had the script again, I dispatched it to a company that *advertised* for book manuscripts. I suspected that it was a firm of "vanity" publishers, but I had lost faith in my novel after reading it through, and thought I would at least find out how this company functioned.

Their methods were quite simple. First of all, they returned the "return" postage that *I* had sent along with the script (more than a dollar back, right there!), and a letter informed me that my work would be given prompt consideration. It was, for within a week they wrote again, praising the book just to the right degree, and not overdoing it to the extent that I would suspect their sincerity. But . . . the way things were, their lists being full at the moment, etc., the way matters stood they did not see how they could take the full risk without some guarantee. . . . In short, did I have any money, and if so, about how much? The letter continued to say that I would have to underwrite only a *part* of the publication costs, perhaps, and it would be a shame if so excellent a book was not published, and so on, and so on. I hastily replied that I had no money.

Still they did not return the manuscript. Another letter came, asking if I had friends. Perhaps I could find backing . . .

I wrote again, saying that I thought I could get William Allan White to back the book. Only they could write to Emporia and do the asking. This letter brought the manuscript home again. I don't know what happened to it after that—I might have destroyed it, but I think I simply moved away from it somewhere. I don't even remember its title.

But I have no regrets. Writing it was an experience, and trying to have it published was another.

It might be asked—as one radio roundtabler says to another, "I'm glad you asked that"—if an arrangement in which an author publishes at his own expense doesn't sometimes work out. It has happened, of course, that a self-issued book has attracted attention—enough attention to secure a legitimate publisher for the author's next book; but unless the author has money to throw around, he had best leave the publishing to those who know the publishing business. If his book will sell, if it is worthwhile, he will find a firm who will print it and who will pay him his share of the profits of that book. Even if the book isn't worthwhile, he might find a publisher who will take the risk. And because of the publisher's knowledge and skill—and the use of advertising—the doubtful book might even make money. But it's certain that in such a case the writer would wind up fearfully in the hole if he tried to have the book manufactured at his own expense.

If the writer can afford it and he is thinking of something aside from profits, he might bring out something of his own in book covers, "privately printed." Book collectors, especially, sometimes do this, book collectors who are writers as well. I have plans of my own for bringing out an Ambrose Bierce item, in an edition of a hundred copies or so. It will have to be a slim little book, and even so, I expect to lose a little money.

CHAPTER 8
General Grant Slept Here

BLACK HAWK, COLO. LOOKING UP LEFT FORK TOWARD CENTRAL CITY, COLO.

10. Black Hawk, Colorado, ca. 1920s. The surrounding mines and ghost towns became a staple of Paul's early fiction. *Author's collection.*

W riting the novel had put me behind financially, for even the limited amount of material I turned out for *The Laugh Factory* was below my usual average and a smaller percentage of it was accepted. Not wanting to admit to Montague that I had been writing an unsuccessful novel, I explained it by saying that I had "lost some of my enthusiasm" for joke writing. He immediately replied, telling me how important enthusiasm was and that I should do my best to hold on to it. Of course, what really happened was that I had gone a little stale from overwork; a tired or worried mind can't be expected to come through with anything very clever or original, and when forced or whipped, it has a tendency to balk altogether, as many a brain worker who has experimented with alcohol has sooner or later discovered. At this period of my life I wasn't fooling with John Barleycorn, and recuperation came quickly. As soon as we had the necessary money, we moved again, this time leaving Kansas and returning to the twin mining camps of Black Hawk and Central City.

Living in a ghost town is an interesting experience. While food was expensive because of transportation difficulties, rent was almost nothing. In this camp hundreds of houses stood empty, many of them in a state of more or less ruin, of course; but there were dozens that, if moved to Denver, would have rented for forty or fifty dollars a month. During my two years in this district we occupied two houses at different times, both furnished, and the rent was hardly more than the light and water bill. A friend of mine bought a fine brick house by paying the delinquent taxes, which amounted to less than two hundred dollars.

"Ghost towns might be very fascinating to visit," friends of mine have said, "but to live in one—awful! Isn't it terribly depressing? Two or three hours of it would be enough to satisfy me."

But the glow of romance that hung over the old "diggings" never faded for me, although the idea of spending my life there wasn't very inviting. It would be, I think, more than a little depressing to grow old in a ghost town, with everything falling into deterioration and decay along with you. Still, a great many people have been born, have lived, and died in such camps as Central and Cripple Creek and Leadville, and no doubt many still will do so. First the depression, the price of gold and then the war have revived these districts. Shortly after I left Central City, the town was discovered by the art-minded, and drama holds sway again in the old opera house every summer. Tourists and visitors from Denver began swarming through—not "in" but "through"—and probably much of the rusted, rotting glamour has gone from it. When I was there, summer visitors were rare, and in winter nonexistent.

As I had spent much of my childhood in Black Hawk, the natives accepted me as one of their own, and I soon knew almost everyone in tiny, almost mile-high Gilpin County. Nearly every day I would go exploring, visiting crumbling and sometimes almost inaccessible mine shacks, clambering over discolored "dumps" of waste rock, often taking a Winchester with me and knocking over a snowshoe rabbit or two on the way home. There were many queer characters. The gold-mining country has a higher proportion of hermits, I think, than any other. Once in a while one of these lonely, brooding old men became insane.

One day I called at the post office for the mail of a friend, and received several rolled-up newspapers and a letter. The latter bore a local postmark, was addressed in a peculiar scrawl—and it smelled. I stayed with my friend until he opened it. Inside the envelope was a letter filled with badly spelled threats and obscenities, and a photogravure page torn from a Denver paper. This pictured native Africans in scanty costume, and the sender had penciled heavy Xs on their loin-cloths. Both letter and enclosure were wrinkled, and daubed with filth. It was obvious that intimate use had been made of them before they were sealed into the envelope.

My friend sputtered when he saw all this, and didn't know whether to swear or to laugh. But I did, and couldn't help it, though my mirth became more restrained when I realized that we weren't dealing with a Rabelaisian practical joker but with a man who was very sick mentally. A posse carrying re-volvers and rifles was sent to capture the poor fellow—the sheriff and all the prominent men of the camp had received similar communications—but I am glad to say that he was taken into custody without much of a struggle.

Loneliness alone doesn't drive people insane, of course; the men who deliberately live apart from their fellows are of-ten unbalanced to begin with. Not that prospectors are crazy as a class—the great majority are as level-headed as anyone else, and they show a marvelous shrewdness in getting grub-stakes for themselves. One old character, "Uncle Johnny," used to call on me regularly.

"Hey, P—a—w—l!" he would shout as he came up the canyon steps. He had been deafened in a powder blast and thought everyone else had suffered the same accident.

"Well, what do you think o' *this*?" he would roar, throwing some ore specimens onto the kitchen table. Although I was no mineralogist I would always examine the fragments with a great appearance of wisdom.

"Looks pretty good!" I would scream.

"Good, did you say?" was his yell, swaying before me with a thin hand cupped around his ear. "It's goddam good! It's better than the Silver Queen! I located the Silver Queen in 1889! Sold 'er for twenty thousand and she brought in a mil-lion! I want you to take this up to Central and get it assayed,

Pawl! Assayed! I ain't got the money! You get it assayed and have the report here next time I come! You'll get a share! Yessir, a goddam good share!"

"How about a bite to eat before you go?"

"Well, I ain't hongry, but—thanks, I might get somethin' down!"

He would eat pancakes like a famished wolf, and after he had stuffed his pockets and gunny sack with whatever else could be spared, he would disappear for another two or three weeks. Then he would show up with another handful of rocks.

"Pawl! Let's see the assay slip of that last bunch of specimens!"

I would have to tell him that I hadn't been up to Central, that I had forgotten about the ore, or that I had been too short myself to pay the assaying fee.

"Well, it's don't matter because these specimens are away to hell-and-gone better than the last! Yessir! Just look at the horn silver in these! This is better stuff than ever came out of the guts of the Queen! I located the Queen in 1889!"

"Fine, but how about a bite to eat?"

"I might get somethin' down. But you get an assay on these specimens! The next time I see you—"

Uncle Johnny wasn't stalling about the assays; he really wanted them made, and he wasn't deceiving anyone. He had really discovered the Silver Queen, and I hope, if he's still living, that he has found another one. If he did, I'm sure that those who helped him along with food, dynamite, and "assays" weren't forgotten. Mining-camp people are usually willing to grubstake a prospector in whom they have confidence; they remember that H. A. W. Tabor got his start by risking groceries in that way. The mining-camp storekeepers sometimes allow an amazing amount of credit—in Black Hawk I once saw an account of more than a thousand dollars. The debtor had no assets except a pick, a shovel, and an old reputation for being lucky.

A writer's limit of credit, I discovered, was very considerably lower.

Whenever I wandered up Apex Canyon I would stop in for a chat with Mr. O'Rae. This old gentleman had an education at the University of Dublin that had not altogether decayed, and while he lived as a recluse, I believe he enjoyed my visits, for I let him do all the talking, which, as a Westerner would put it, was a plumb whole lot. I would be mentally exhausted upon leaving, for his extensive vocabulary was interlarded with bits of Gaelic and with English words not often used in ordinary conversation. "Indubitably" was one of his favorites, and I liked the way it rolled off his tongue. Mr. O'Rae lived upon a small remittance from an almost-defunct mining company whose property he was supposed to keep an eye on, and he had a little mine of his own, too, in his backyard. He did not live alone, exactly; his house was alive with prancing and fluttering white pigeons. One had to be careful where he sat down, for Mr. O'Rae's furniture was as splattered as statues of General Grant.

A ghost town, strictly speaking, is one that has been completely abandoned and that has no inhabitants at all. Nevadaville, above Central City, could almost qualify, for it had once had a population of more than a thousand, and now it had just one citizen. This dead settlement with its clusters of buildings, an almost modern firehouse, and saloons with pool tables still in them stood just as it had in the 1880s, as if the thin air of the nine-thousand-foot altitude had preserved it. I liked to rummage through the old, deserted houses, being particularly interested in dusty letters and documents of ancient mining days.

Once I nearly had my head blown off. Near the center of the old town I came upon a promising house, a frame cottage with a covered porch at the rear. The door of this was open, and I could see evidence of burros having strayed into it for shelter—or out of sheer cussedness. Stepping over their deposits, I tried the knob of the door leading into the house itself; it yielded, and I found myself in a well-furnished but very dusty room.

"It looks as if the owner might have only moved out yesterday," I thought, as I went through the musty place. There was bedding piled onto a four-poster in one red-papered room; there were all sorts of little knickknacks that would do for souvenirs, and on the table was a cloth covered with a dark stain that I persuaded myself to be blood.

"Some poor miner had a hemorrhage while sitting in this chair, years ago," I reconstructed, shivering a little. "Then he stumbled into that room yonder, and died on that bed. If there were such things as ghosts, this place would sure be haunted."

There might be the makings of a short story here, I decided as I walked in circles through the sinister rooms, never keeping my back long turned in the same direction. Suppose the man had been murdered, slain for his gold . . .

My nerves began to get a bit on edge, so I gathered up an armful of relics and started out of the house. When a man with a gun suddenly loomed up before me, I stood petrified, too startled to run.

"Of all the goshdurned brass I ever saw! What do you mean, robbin' my house right in broad daylight?" shrilled a thin man with a thick mustache. I was facing the town's lone inhabitant.

"*Your* house?" I gulped. "Why, I didn't know anybody lived here! This is *your* house?"

"Of course it is! You're a thief, that's what you are, and I've caught you red-handed!"

I explained that I had supposed the place to have been long deserted, as were all the other houses in Nevadaville. This added to the man's indignation, for he was the mayor, he said, of the town, and it would soon come back in a bigger boom than ever. In the meantime he was standing guard over it, and I had no right to touch *anything* anywhere in it. He was not only the mayor, but the police and fire departments as well. How I ever managed to talk him out of it, I don't know, but finally I dropped my booty and fled. A queer predicament, I thought, if he had locked me in the Nevadaville calaboose. The mayor had a lot of civic pride, and as judge he might have sentenced me to life in order to double the town's population.

The most forlorn addendum to an abandoned settlement is, I think, its burial ground. The ghost of a ghost town, where the dead seem friendless and forgotten. If the dead are ever lonely, these are, for their loved ones will never join them. I wandered once into Nevadaville's graveyard and found it depressing even in daylight, though the aspens were rustling cheerfully enough and the scent of the pines was pleasant. The lives of most of these people had been short, and many had died violently. Reading the epitaphs, I wondered what sort of an anthology a poet like Edgar Lee Masters could have made of them. I remember one little tombstone with a tiny lamb carved in marble. The dates, of forty years before, were pitifully close together, and the name was David Sleep. Before I left the weed-grown place I found myself whispering it over and over—David Sleep. I wanted to write some verses about this unknown child who had lived and died so long before—they would have been pretty mawkish.

Too healthy to haunt cemeteries Edgar Poe fashion, I never went back, but I have often thought of little David, wondering who his parents had been and if they had found enough gold to repay them in roaring old Nevadaville . . .

Level ground for burial plots was at a premium in the mountain country, and Black Hawk's cemetery was several miles away at the top of a hill where the wind was always howling and booming down from the Divide. There were several prospect holes inside the enclosure. Once in a while, in digging a grave, a promising little streak of gold or silver would be struck, and when that happened the grave was made elsewhere and the original excavation feverishly deepened, sometimes, old-timers have told me, with the deceased's funeral indefinitely postponed. Knowing the virulence of the gold fever, I can easily believe it. I once saw a couple of men start digging the foundation for a house, and end up by forming a stock company and selling shares in their unexpectedly rich cellar.

I kept brushing off the gold bug, but it eventually bit me. I became acquainted with Bill Kerrick, the only winter inhabitant of Apex, a little scattering of log cabins, and I spent some weeks up there, traveling about on skis and snowshoes. We were practically marooned there for a while, and for the lack of anything else to do we explored Kerrick's mine. Like everyone else, he had one—I think I was the only resident of the county who hadn't. Bill's tunnel extended four hundred feet into the mountain, and the ore body at the end of it looked very good—he said. He generously offered me a share if I would help raise the necessary money to start the mine going again. We would start a company, and my job would be to write the "literature" and the "chance of a lifetime" letters to the prospective buyers of the stock. I was enthusiastic over the scheme, but fortunately our plans didn't materialize. If they had, federal laws being as they are, I would just be getting released, along about now, from Leavenworth.

During my second year in Black Hawk I reached my peak in the production of short humor. *The Laugh Factory* showed signs of folding up (it suspended not long after), and by wriggling out of my "contract" to a certain extent I was able to sell consistently to *Life* and received a regular weekly check, which sometimes amounted to sixty dollars or more.

It has been claimed that the *New Yorker* put an end to the "two-liner" or "He and She" joke, and that this magazine was the first to popularize the type of cartoon, now so familiar, that bears one line of comment, or none at all. The old *Life*, however, was traveling in that direction long before the *New Yorker*'s debut. At this period I was selling more "ideas for illustration" than jokes or epigrams, receiving from six to eight dollars each for these, and a little more when the suggestion could be used for *Life*'s cover picture.

While I wasn't aware of it, this foremost American humor magazine was on its way out, and, although it lasted some time longer, the publishers must have been making strenuous efforts in those days. One of the new features that were started was "Neighborhood News," a two-page layout that gave a country newspaper slant to items from various cities throughout the country. Franklin P. Adams was the New York "correspondent." One of his newsy bits was the following:

W. E. Woodward is still working away at his biography of General U. S. Grant but we would rather read a paper-covered life of Lillian Russell than the life of General Grant in full morocco.

Neal R. O'Hera, from Boston, sent in these nifties:

Mrs. F. C. Church Jr. (nee Vanderbilt, christened Muriel) is dusting off her shack at Newport for early occupancy.

The senior class at Harvard are having their photographs taken this week.

This gives a general idea of "Neighborhood News." John Forbes represented Philadelphia; Leslie Roberts reported Montreal; F. P. Armstrong, Jacksonville, Florida; Robert Lord wrote the Hollywood lowdown; Tupper Greenwald, Cincinnati; Asia Kagowan was the name signed to Chicago news; and Elmer C. Adams took care of Detroit.

My assignment was to have been Denver. However, I wrote to Mr. A. M. Sherwood Jr., the associate editor in charge of the new feature, and asked if I couldn't write up the little town of Idaho Springs instead. It had a population of less than a thousand and was out of place among the larger cities, but I thought it would be amusing to include it for that very reason, and Mr. Sherwood agreed. I wrote the copy without troubling to go over the mountain to "Idaho," simply taking some items from the local paper and fixing them up a bit:

Senator and Mrs. Reashaw drove over a cliff en route to Denver recently.

Rumor has it that Courtney R. Cooper is in the East, gathering material for a new Western novel.

The Denver papers copied these and other Idaho Springs items, giving *Life* some advertising. Had these been under a Denver dateline they would probably have gone unnoticed.

At this time I was selling to *Film Fun, College Humor*, and others. Among the editors who wrote encouraging letters was N. L. Pines, then only an assistant, I think. He is now the president of a company publishing more than fifty magazines.

It was still fiction that I wanted to be writing, and once again, for a variety of reasons, I became discouraged with my lot as a joke writer. The art department of the *Chicago Daily News* suddenly announced that they were no longer in the market for fillers. Their checks had been small, but more certain than any others, and I was disheartened. *Judge* had accepted a good deal of my material, and some of it had been published, but I was still waiting for payment. Other worries didn't help my work; I had domestic troubles that quickly ended in divorce, and in a mental slump I left Black Hawk, moving a couple of miles up the mountain to Central City.

Haven't I already mentioned General Ulysses S. Grant in this chapter? Strangely enough, I now found myself making my home in the general's suite at the Teller House. This once-famous hotel had been built by Senator Henry Teller, and at this time it was being operated by his son, who, like the house, was still living in the glorious, gold-misted past. Only four or five rooms of the tall, gaunt building were occupied, and I was assigned to the rooms overlooking the street above the lobby where, I was told, Grant had been entertained half a century before. I was charged, I think, four dollars a week for the apartment, which, I suspect, was more than the general had paid. According to the stories told in Central, some of them apocryphal, he was right royally entertained on his visit to the camp. One old-timer was positive that a paving of silver dollars had been laid down, from the curb to the doors of the Teller, for the distinguished guest to walk upon.

"'Twasn't silver dollars, at all!" another resident snorted indignantly. "It was double eagles—twenty dollar gold pieces. Silver dollars—phooo! It was them pikers in Leadville that put down the silver."

My rooms were rather gloomy, for the woodwork and ornately carved furniture were dark with age, and the wallpaper was somber, peeling a little in spots. Under the musty magnificence of the bed was a formidable piece of pottery, elaborately flowered and gilded. It would have made an interesting souvenir, but the general hadn't autographed it, unfortunately, and Mr. Teller wouldn't give me a certificate of authenticity.

If I were to write short stories, burning my joke-writing bridge behind me, this was the place! "I'll fight it out on this line," I told the dim, bearded face in the tall mirror—it was not my face, there was a cigar in it—"if it takes all summer."

CHAPTER 9
Enter Mr. Oliphant

11. The pulp writer, ca. 1931. *Collection of Patricia Binkley.*

My campaign, and its terms of unconditional surrender, was directed at Street & Smith, then the leader in the pulp field, although the newer firm of Fiction House and others were pressing this old company very hard for supremacy. I chose Street & Smith because of its long publishing record and its reputation of prompt payment at a minimum rate of one cent a word. I had seen enough of their rejection slips, and was tired of looking at pictures of their unlovely office building. I wanted to see what their checks were like. After studying over their string, I decided to shoot at *Wild West Weekly*.

This magazine had been established in 1902, but after a long suspension had just resumed publication. Its format was good, if rather slender; it featured a "Billy West" novelette and several short stories. "Billy West and his pards," I was to learn, were revamped characters resurrected from the old magazine, when Billy was known as "Young Wild West" and who gave the magazine its name. The stories were signed by Cleve Endicott, and if there was ever such a person, he wrote before I was born. Several writers took turns at writing the long "Billy West on Circle J" series and I was to write many of them myself, combined with characters of my own creation. The adventures of Billy West, his cowhands Joe Scott and Buck Foster, and Sing Lo, the cook, went on and on, but each story was complete in itself and did not irritate the reader by being "continued." At the same time, the reader could look forward to reading more about his favorites. This arrangement was new to me, and I thought the idea a good one. Of course, A. Conan Doyle's Sherlock Holmes stories had been written along that same general pattern—the same two central characters, Holmes and Watson, appearing over and over again. If I had thought about it I would have recognized the device as an ancient one. Writers have even used a single locality, as Alfred Henry Lewis did in the Wolfville series, have peopled it with characters, and have written about it until they, and their readers, were tired of it. How long, I wondered, could a reader be *kept* interested?

Writing a story of about three thousand words and entitling it "The Whispering Gunman," I sent it to *Wild West*, and while waiting to hear from it, wrote several others. As the magazine appeared every week, it would use a large amount of material, and if I could sell to it consistently my present financial worries should be over.

Street & Smith had always been cold in their dealings, it had seemed to me, for I had never received so much as a penciled notation on a rejection slip in return for the dozens of scripts I had sent them a couple of years earlier. So when a letter came from the editor of *Wild West*, saying that my story was being "considered" for publication, and would I please tell him something about myself, I was in a fever. The letter was signed Ronald Oliphant. It was the first time I had seen that signature; it was to become very familiar to me during the next dozen years.

The first little story was bought and immediately paid for at a cent per word. My next two stories were returned with brief letters explaining why, but before I had time to become discouraged again, the fourth yarn sold, and I received another of Street & Smith's checks, this time for forty-five dollars. In those days, their checks were very elaborately printed, in color, and pictured their building again, this time the entrance doorway, which was much lovelier than the bleak view furnished by their rejection slips.

Every magazine has its "policy" and taboos, and Mr. Oliphant's were well defined. The heroes should be young

Americans, and mustn't drink, although they could smoke cigarettes. No out-and-out profanity was to be used, even by the villain of the piece, though the swearing could be implied. The love interest, if used, should be soft-pedaled, and all women were "good." Instead of using the word "blood," the writer was required to make use of an euphemism such as "crimson" or "scarlet." This had to "flow" or otherwise issue from a wound, as the victim could not "bleed." The hero could kill people pretty freely, but always in self-defense, or in the defense of others weaker than himself, and he could never take an unfair advantage of the villain, no matter what depended on it. The hero should get out of trouble through his own ingenuity and not through the long arm of coincidence. *Wild West* was aimed at the younger reader and his less-sophisticated elders. It was to be of the "old" West, with none of the modernities (such as Ford cars, automatic pistols, airplanes, dope, and immigrant smuggling) that marred so many of the Western magazines—in Mr. Oliphant's opinion, and in mine. I also agreed that we could appeal to young readers without "writing down" or being "juvenile," and that with a simple, vigorous style a writer could do good work and still keep within the limitations.

After learning *Wild West*'s requirements, I sold every story I submitted until Mr. Oliphant relinquished the editorship in the 1940s. Only two, I think, were returned to me for revision, and these were purchased on the next trip.

When I had sold Oliphant a dozen stories in quick succession, he wrote and asked my permission to put some of them under what he called "house pen names." I was going to be a big producer, he explained, and this arrangement would enable him to print more than one of my stories at a time. Anything that would accomplish that, I decided, was all right with me, and from that time onward much of my work appeared under the names of Ward M. Stevens, Andrew A. Griffin, Phillip F. Deere, Dean McKinley, and others. In a short time Ward M. Stevens became exclusively "me" and most of my stories appeared under it.

I was soon asked to write a novelette of from twelve to fifteen thousand words, and as it was successful I began concentrating on these longer lengths. Novelettes, for me at least, were easier to write than short stories. There is more room to work in, a better chance to develop the characters. And of course $150 for two or three days' work was real money, at least to me.

The idea of a "series" character kept recurring to me. Short stories dealing with "The Whistling Kid" and "The Ranny Kid" were appearing regularly, and the late J. Allan Dunn had "Bud Jones" showing up every week or two. What I wanted to do was a series of novelettes. The magazine had now been enlarged and, with the excellent covers by H. W. Scott, had become as attractive as any on the newsstands. It seemed a good one to tie to.

In the fall I returned to the old hometown in Kansas, stopping in Denver to buy myself a tremendous Cadillac; an open car painted a pale gray. This was my idea at the time of "cutting a swath" and showing the townfolk how mistaken they had been about me. None of the natives had ever owned a Cadillac, some had never seen one, and to use a localism, I considered myself *some* punkins. However, nobody wanted to hit the chin I stuck out. The folks were only mildly interested. Making a fool of myself is a habit I haven't conquered to this day. It's surprising how many ways there are of doing it.

However, during the winter, while feeling and trying to sow my oats, I did get quite a lot of work accomplished. In a novelette, "The Gunman of Old Monterey," I introduced a character I called Kid Wolf. He was a two-gun man, spoke with a Texas drawl, and dressed in fringed buckskins. In addition, he carried a bowie knife in a concealed sheath sewn inside his shirt collar, and this was his "ace in the hole." When his enemies had him apparently at their mercy, he would draw and hurl the knife with uncanny accuracy at his victim's throat. His friends called him "The Kid," but the wrongdoers of the West learned to know him by his last name. A lover of justice, he and his big white horse, Blizzard, traveled about looking for wrongs to right and a chance to battle for the "undah dawg" whenever he found oppression. This "Soldier of Misfortune" seemed to me to have possibilities, and when I sent in the first Kid Wolf story, I suggested writing a series of novelettes dealing with the tall, handsome, always courteous gentleman from Texas. Oliphant replied that he was afraid he already had too many series about "Kids." However, shortly after the novelette was printed, he advised me that many readers had written in about it asking for more, and he gave me the "go ahead" on a string of Kid Wolf yarns, a string that was unbroken until the magazine itself was forced to suspend publication in the winter of 1943 for the duration of the war. In all, I must have written between one and two million words about Mr. Wolf. A closer estimate would give me and my readers a headache.

Now that I was a professional writer of Westerns, I began to realize that there was much about Western life I didn't know, much that I couldn't get by reading. I was fairly familiar with miners and mining, but the prince of the Western was, and will continue to be, the cowboy. Although his environment was rapidly changing, he wasn't yet extinct, and I made up my mind to look him up. One bitter February day I adjusted the curtains of my automobile and started toward southern Arizona.

After bucking snow through Kansas, Oklahoma, and the Panhandle I struck sunshine of a most peculiar and wondrous kind, and stayed in it. It is traitorous of a California resident to say so, but the Southwest, and particularly Arizona, has the best winter climate in the country. I can't recommend the summers so highly, but I spent several hot seasons there and found it endurable enough in spite of very high thermometer readings.

Making the long drive from El Paso to Tucson in one day, I arrived in the evening and awoke the next morning to find myself on a different planet. I had always thought of the desert as a drab and empty waste of sand and sagebrush, but this country—well, it was as beautiful as the Arizona Chamber of Commerce said it was, which, of course, was going some. The desert was covered with flowers at this time of year; the cacti were beginning to throw out strange blooms of many colors, and the long wands of the ocotillas were tipped with red candle flames. The giant saguaro was the weirdest plant of all, and yet even it put on a flowered hat. The deadly spined cholla, the paloverde, the lluvia d'oro—nearly every plant was new to me. So was everything else.

Tucson was crowded, for the annual fiesta and rodeo would soon be held, but luckily I found a room off the patio at the old Willard Hotel, across from the library and two blocks from Congress Street. I made the place my headquarters, finding friendly people in charge (the Andersons), and installed my typewriter not far from the horsiest and cowiest lobby in Pima County. Most of the professional ropers, riders, and bulldoggers roomed there while waiting for the rodeo (pronounced ro-DAY-o in the Southwest) to get under way. In addition, ranchers and stock buyers used the Willard for a rendezvous, and it was there I met the late Ted Smith, Ed Ryan, and other well-known Tucsonians. "Dooley" Bookman, who later became a friend of Kate Smith's, was a friend of mine. But then, he was that way toward all, and when he died not so long ago, all Tucson mourned. His business? He had a pool hall and sold tobacco and curios. Dooley was also something else—but then, Kate Smith has told his story better than I can.

Mexico was having the last of its interesting and bloody *revoluciones* that winter. As usual, the fighting was principally in the northern frontier states, and with a couple of the more adventurous Willard guests I drove down to the border below Bisbee where a battle was in progress. The fighting centered about the little town of Naco, which is half in Arizona, half in Sonora, with a wire fence between.

We parked as close to the festivities as the American Border Patrol would allow, and managed to walk in much nearer, joining some curious Bisbeeites in the mesquite. Now and then a bullet would whisk across and throw up a puff of United States dust, which seemed to make our border patrolmen peevish. One faction had torn up the railroad track, and the other (it wasn't clear which side was which) was rebuilding it ahead of a military train that was creeping around the base of the great mountain south of the town. Rails that the train had just passed over would be picked up and laid down in front of the engine, which would then move up another few yards, and then the track-laying would be repeated, with everyone shooting enthusiastically. There was no artillery in evidence, and the appearance of an biplane over the town spoiled the picture: somehow it didn't belong in it. We heard that it had dropped explosives that morning, and that an old Mexican woman had been killed.

"Bombs falling on North American soil—I'm not sure that I like it," said one of my companions, Al Immel of Joplin, Missouri. "You know what? Those Mexicans are going to fool around until revolutions won't be any fun anymore."

That evening we drove on east to Douglas, and managed to cross the Mexican line into Agua Prieta. This town was in the hands of the rebels, they having seized the customhouse, the banks, and the cantinas, probably in reverse order. We entered one of the latter and immediately became the paying guests of a group of revolutionary officers, none of which were below the rank of colonel. It was quite a party, with plenty of *sotol, mescal, and tequila* (liquid fire of three different temperature ranges). Things became rather misty before morning, but I remember that we despised Gil and hated Calles. We drank to Obregon's memory or perhaps to Obregon's assassin, and I was introduced to a general who I was assured was to be the next governor of Sonora; perhaps, *quien sabe*, even *presidente* of all Mexico. His Excellency made a deprecatory gesture that meant, in any language, "Alas, I am only in the hands of my friends." Shortly afterward, the officers genially began explaining the mechanisms of their Lugers and Mausers, and we thought it time to go. Back in Tucson a few days later, we read that our Agua Prieta *amigos* had been captured and stood against the customary adobe wall.

Later that year, the *Tucson Citizen* wrote up, in a humorous fashion, a *Wild West Weekly* yarn that I had written about Deputy Sheriff John Farrell. In a column and a half of type the paper quoted excepts from the novelette, which I had called "The Ace of Colts." The article ended:

> Now the real John Farrell is well known to Tucson folk. For two years he has been deputy sheriff, and prior to that time he served for five years with the Border Patrol. He was born and reared in Santa Cruz county, in the Harshaw District, near Patagonia. . . . "Farrell is a very efficient officer," Sheriff McDonald said. "I consider him one of the best in the State of Arizona. He takes a great interest in his work, and hours mean nothing to him. . . . I consider him a man of exceptionally good judgment." When asked as to Johnny's prowess with a gun, the sheriff replied: "Johnny is plenty good with a gun."

This write-up nearly got me into trouble with Ronald Oliphant, who wrote from New York that I had better be very careful when I used the names of real persons in my stories. In this case, maybe it was all right, he said, but it would be best not to do it again, as Street & Smith had faced lawsuits as a result of similarity of names. It was well, he added, that I had made the deputy the hero of my piece and not the villain.

I had become acquainted with Johnny Farrell at the Willard. He was all the sheriff said he was, and a dashing young fellow besides. But one night, after we had partaken of a jolt or two of Tucson Lightning, he twirled his stag-handled Colt

.45 on his finger and announced that he could and would shoot the cigarette out of my mouth. This was no improvement, it seemed to me, on the more usual Western pleasantry of banging away at a tenderfoot's heels, and I demurred—rapidly. I told him I would get even by putting him in a blood-and-thunder story; he seemed pleased at the idea, and "The Ace of Colts" was the result. I *tried* not to make Johnny a hero, but while writing the yarn I couldn't forget the glint of that stag-handled gun.

In between the Kid Wolf novelettes, I was writing so-called independents such as the just mentioned one, and I had the formula pretty well in hand by this time. Arizona had got under my skin, and a little of its color was bound to creep into my work. I couldn't have kept it out if I'd tried. One of the independents I wrote that summer was called "The Eleventh Notch," and it dealt with a "good" outlaw. As I was still writing about him in 1943, fourteen years later, I'll give away my secret—if any. I had discovered that the hunted always received more reader sympathy than the hunter. The Billy the Kid legend was proof enough of that. In spite of the murderous character of that most famous of all Western gunmen, the people had taken him to their hearts. In New Mexico, to be sure, a large faction sided with Pat Garrett, the sheriff who killed Billy, but they *did* take sides in a matter that had ended half a century before, and many were the arguments I heard pro and con. Despite of all the evidence I had read and sifted, and which pretty conclusively showed that William Bonney (the Kid) was the vicious killer his bucktoothed photograph portrays, I had a sneaking admiration for him too. His life, especially as told by Walter Noble Burns, makes those of the James boys, the Youngers, and the Daltons pretty humdrum.

In "The Eleventh Notch" I developed a character along Billy the Kid lines, but without the repellent traits of the real person. I called my hero Sonny Tabor. The Jolson "talkie" *Sonny Boy* was being shown in Tucson that week, and it's likely the suggestion for the first name came from that, and Tabor from the Colorado Tabors. I made his age "about twenty," although he looked younger because of his deceptively harmless manner, his innocent blue eyes, and the bullet scar in his tanned cheek, which "resembled a dimple." Of course, he was a whiz with his brace of .45s, but like Kid Wolf he was reluctant to take advantage, and when forced to fire upon his lawmen pursuers he took care to aim for their gun arms or shoulders (not plausible, of course, but editors don't want the heroes to kill law officers, no matter what the circumstances). The outlaw had to have a horse, so I gave him a smallish black-and-white pinto named, not very originally, Paint.

The story seemed to have pleased the readers of *Wild West Weekly*, for Oliphant received many letters about it, and he suggested that I go right on with my outlaw. I didn't find it difficult. It's said that the reader puts himself in the hero's place, and while writing about Sonny, I *was* Sonny. I was just immature enough mentally to be able to do it thoroughly and completely. Tabor also was for the underdog, and he righted wrongs whenever he found them, which was in every story. His adventures weren't simply a series of escapes from the manhunters who were after him. I tried to make it evident that he had been outlawed "through no fault of his own," though I wasn't specific as to the original charges against him. He was especially popular when he helped others, which proves, if readers do identify themselves with the leading character, that the readers of *Wild West* were fundamentally a pretty good sort. To this day, I have a soft spot in my heart for Sonny, who has earned me, to date, more than twenty-five thousand dollars.

In Arizona I had found some romance of my own, and that summer I married a Tucson girl, the one who will still be with me, I hope, when the last story is written and the dust cover is dropped over the old typewriter.

CHAPTER 10

Tricks of the Trade

12. The Cadillac that carried Paul from Kansas to Tucson in 1929. *Collection of Patricia Binkley.*

The next year was spent in southern California. A writer can work locked up in a dungeon if necessary; it doesn't make much difference where he does his writing if his mind is free and well stocked. But I think it helps to get around, and I seldom stay more than a year or two in one locality, perhaps because of some inborn restlessness rather than any real need for a change of scene. One of the wisest cracks in a recent movie was: "California? That's the place where nothing ever happens and all of a sudden you're sixty years old." But if there is a narcotic in the California climate it's a pleasant one and, like the tobacco habit, kills lots of octogenarians.

Ronald Oliphant and I were now as well acquainted as we could have been with the width of the continent between us. He edited several magazines, such as *Sport Story* and *Top-Notch*, as well as the weekly, most of the time all at once, but he never seemed to lack the time and patience to point out my literary faults and make useful suggestions . . . something not easy to do in my case, for one of my faults is a tendency to resent criticism. Most writers are introverts, to use a very tired expression. They are a little suspicious of others, over-estimate themselves (or go to the other extreme and dive off into the melancholia of inferiority), and are difficult to handle all around. They are, however, very responsive to praise. Suspicious of what they might think to be flattery, mind you, but downright hungry for encouragement. I know that I do my best work after a few kind words; even though I might pretend otherwise, my spirits zoom when someone tells me that he liked something I have written. Oliphant soon knew me very well: he knew just how to throw me back into high gear when my work showed signs of becoming labored.

The late Alexander Woollcott mentioned the "chronic suspicion of authors that most editors are not quite bright." I have been in contact—and recently, too—with editors who didn't seem to know a good thing when they saw it; none are infallible, and the blind spots of some (sub-editors in most cases) are enormous. On the whole, however, they are cooperative to the best of their abilities, and their job, as is the author's, is to please the public. If I dwell on Ronald Oliphant at some length, it's because he typifies the editorial link between writer and reader when at its best. I might use some other editor as an example. . . . I know other good ones; but every writer has his favorite. Some didn't like Oliphant, of course. Especially those who couldn't sell him as much as they thought they ought.

Some random extracts from his letters might be of interest, and possibly of help, to other writers, or to those who would like to "cash in" on the pulps:

I am purchasing this story but I think it moves a little TOO fast. While reading it one gets the same impression as when a movie film is being too rapidly cranked. Use some of the baseball pitcher's change of pace. Give the reader time to catch his breath between the exciting episodes and they will be more effective.[1]

One thing about the story that I didn't care for was its excessive brutality. This is something you are inclined to overdo at times—making the scenes raw and brutal, even to the point of disgusting the reader. I know that this is difficult to avoid sometimes, when you are striving to write episodes that will thrill the reader. I refer particularly to the incident when the man kills the mother dog and her pups with the axe.[2]

I replied to this—trying to justify myself, as usual—that Saunders's book, *Beautiful Joe*, contained a similar scene, and that the brutality evidently hadn't shocked the many generations of children who had read it. But you can't argue with an editor!

The Alaskan story you suggested writing is a little off trail for us, as our chief setting for stories is the wild West era and area of the country. I would hardly care to have a cover length story, that is 15,000 words, with that setting. I know you like to write that sort of thing once in a while and we have run them occasionally, but I would be inclined to set the limit at 12,000 words on such a story. I think you will appreciate the reasons for this.[3]

I guess you win on the question of mochila versus pouch. No doubt both were used at different times and places. Personally, I never rode the pony mail, so I don't know what they carried, and have to depend on such authorities as Arthur Chapman, Buffalo Bill and others. The ways of the Butterfield Line were different, it seems, than those of the Overland.[4]

Just a word of warning. It seems to me that you are running a little too much toward conversational openings in some of your recent stories. I noticed this particularly in the new "king kolt" novelette, and also in "Sonny Tabor's Maverick Guns." The characters seem to talk around quite a bit before the story really gets going or the first incident is introduced.[5]

Referring to Page 25, paragraph 5, of "Sonny Tabor's Showdown" which I am purchasing this week, it is always the policy of this magazine to have bad hombres kidnap nice young girls only for mercenary motives of ransom, and not for motives which might in this day and age be construed as coming under the Mann Act. Savvy? As you have the paragraph originally, the intent and purpose of the bad hombre is plainly—well, not mercenary. Need I say more? We have amended the paragraph to read as shown by the enclosed memo. I thought I had mentioned this before. If not, it's my own fault I have to type this letter myself so as not to embarrass the stenog.[6]

As for the stenog, I think Mr. Oliphant was pulling my leg. A New York stenog, too!

I am wondering if you received my letter of July 24th, asking you to work on a Thanksgiving Kid Wolf novelette of 15,000 words to be ready by August 27th? If you didn't get my letter, would you mind digging into it right away, as it is now due at the Art Department? You know the usual ingredients that they like for Thanksgiving—lots of human interest. If you have to start the story now, would you please choose a suitable cover scene for the artist to work on, and send it as soon as you have it figured out?[7]

This sometimes happened. I'd have to think of an appropriate scene for the cover, then work the scene into the forthcoming story. Sometimes it worked the other way, and the Art Department sent me a blueprint of a cover, and I was supposed to write a story of which it would be suitable.

Just a line in haste to say that I'd rather you wouldn't model your new Mounty series on anything you may read in the current issues of TOP-NOTCH. Just be yourself and write them in the style that you feel is best suited to them. If you need data on the Mounties, the Commissioner, R.C.M.P., Ottawa, Ont., will be glad to send you data, pamphlets, etc. They are pleased to have authors keep the technical details correct.[8]

We like the new Tabor story very much, and it will be purchased this week. However, our credulity was a little strained by that episode on pages 33 and 34 where Paint, with Sonny on his back, jumps into the box car of the moving train. As you truly say in the story: "On the face of it, it seemed impossible." However, I rather think the boys will like it. Do you know if this has ever been done? I suppose the movies have done it at some time or other.[9]

Shortly after the holidays' rush of mail is over, you should receive a package with express charges collect. This will contain the original oil painting of Sonny Tabor and his horse Paint, the reproductions of which will be given away as premiums to readers . . . this is not a Christmas gift, but rather what the author of Alice in Wonderland would call an "unchristmas present." It so happened that the art department was having a grand round-up of the pictures, and I spotted this one, and knowing you would like it, I brought my powerful influence to bear . . . but the Art Editor was hard-hearted and would not agree to pay the express charges. Anyway, I hope you will enjoy having the picture.[10]

This painting was by Tom Lovell. The portrait of Kid Wolf was painted by H. W. Scott.

Now feller, you asked for it, and now I am going to give you the well known pep talk. We thought the last Sonny Tabor yarn was a little flat, and in the independent "Runt Madigan . . . Gun Lawyer" it seemed to us that Runt would have had a sweet time getting out of his difficulties had it not been for Shorty's dying confession. In other words, the plotting of the story seemed a little careless and you seemed to take the line of least resistance in finding a way out. I realize that it is very hard to write again and again about the same characters, but I think we can keep up the standard if you will try to avoid the trite or stereotype situations which make it too easy for the hero to clear things up.[11]

Don't worry too much about typographical matters. A great many of these are purely arbitrary. We follow the spellings of Webster's Dictionary, and these, in many cases, differ from the Standard Dictionary. I am afraid it would take your mind off the writing of the story if you paid too much attention to the mechanical details. Your copy is really very good, but of course a copy reader goes over it so as to put it in shape for the printer, and makes it conform to our office style.[12]

I'm glad to learn that . . . Ken Maynard is interested in the Kid Wolf stories. Did I ever tell you that I made strenuous efforts to get Maynard interested in Kid Wolf some time ago, but that I ran up against a stone wall in the person of a Mr. —— who apparently was the typical big-shot movie executive that is so highly satirized? It seemed impossible to accomplish anything at this end through —— who was handling Maynard at the time. I am sending him a copy of the book, and also dropping him a line, and hope that this will accomplish good results.[13]

I had several letters from Mr. Maynard regarding the making of some Kid Wolf pictures, but for some reason none was ever made.

I should like to have a 15,000 word novelette written around an encounter between Sonny Tabor and Sheriff Pete Rice (and his deputies Misery Hicks and Teeny Butler). Would you mind reading over enough of the story "The Sheriff of Buzzard Gap" to familiarize yourself with the characters and locale? I think that this may give you some opportunities for a little variety, as Pete Rice isn't the usual dumb Western sheriff. I should like to have this story by June 10th at the latest. The cover picture gives a pretty good portrait of Pete Rice.[14]

I wrote several of these Pete Rice stories in combination with Tabor. Also some yarns about "The White Wolf," a character that had formerly appeared in *Complete Stories Magazine*. However, I didn't quite like using some other poor writer's brainchildren, though I always tried to do them justice.

I also have a here a very good market for short stories of the business success type—the Horatio Alger stuff brought up to date and better done. The stories should have youthful appeal, with heroes of about eighteen who are making a start in life and gaining the first rungs of the ladder of success. Could you do something of this type?[15]

Who could improve on Horatio Alger? Detesting the idea considerably, I did sell Oliphant several short stories for the new publication; then, to my huge relief, it folded up.

I am returning the final chapter of "Kid Wolf's Committee of Justice" for your revision. Up to the last chapter, the story runs along in the usual smooth manner. It is like many other stories of the series in which the Kid organizes or takes charge of the vigilantes, but that is just what one expects the Kid to do, just as one expects Charlie Chaplin to wear funny shoes and a trick mustache. In the last chapter, however, the Kid and his committee saw down a big cottonwood tree which falls on the villains' cabin so that they have hardly any more chance than if a bomb had been dropped on them from the air. In other words, our hero seems to take an unfair advantage of his foes in order to bring about the ends of Justice. He does not follow his usual method of getting his man in a fair and square fight; the villains are badly injured and at a disadvantage before the fight begins. I would suggest recasting the scene so that the cabin is wrecked without loss of life, chopping down the tree merely serving to bring the villains out into the open for the showdown fight in which Kid Wolf and Jack Claw fight it out. I think you will appreciate the wisdom of making this change.[16]

This sounds as if the story were pretty terrible, and it was. It was revised as Oliphant suggested, and of course for the better. I was always more than willing to do this, as my editor never kept me waiting for my check until the necessary changes were made. He had enough confidence in me to buy the story "muy pronto" and let me make any necessary changes later. But this didn't happen oftener than once every year or two.

"Johnny Forty-five" has just arrived, thanks no doubt to his rugged constitution. I think it would be well for you to use a stronger and heavier manila envelope for your manuscripts. The one containing "Johnny" was badly torn, and I don't really know how the script came through without half of it being lost, or that I didn't receive an empty envelope.[17]

Johnny Forty-five, who was very nearly lost to posterity, became another of my regular characters, and he was still appearing in *Wild West* in 1943, along with his partner and foil, Deputy U.S. Marshal George Krumm. Johnny was a queer little runt, who, although he never smoked, continually rolled and tossed away cigarettes "just to keep his trigger fingers nimble." He also broke out in rhyme at opportune moments, and the readers seemed to like Johnny and kept clamoring for him. Johnny was a lawman; a pursuer, not the pursued, but his cocky manner and the humor of the yarns made him popular. Krumm, who was always getting his young pard in trouble through his pomposities and blunderings, angered many of the readers, who wrote to the editor demanding that Johnny Forty-five appear by himself so as not to be hampered by fat Deputy Krumm's stupidities. Krumm, of course, stayed in, as Johnny's adventures would have suffered without him to complicate matters. I received one letter, though, that caused me some regret over Krumm's character. It was from a young man named Krumm, whose grandfather, George Krumm, and whose father, George Krumm Junior, were both policemen. The boy was much humiliated and demanded that Krumm's name be changed. It was a difficult letter to answer.

It was at about this time, too, or a little later, that I developed another series character, a Pony Express rider, Freckles Malone. He enabled me to use quite a lot of early Western and Indian material, and I kept him going for about six years, until I dropped him in order to bring out still another character, King Kolt, who appeared now and then up to and including 1943. There were others of mine who appeared more than once, but I now had all the series heroes I could manage, and it was quite a job keeping them all going.

One day a letter from England was thrown into my mailbox. It was from the international agency of Curtis Brown and notified me that an English editor had offered four guineas for the British serial rights of "The Whispering Gunman," the first short story of mine that *Wild West Weekly* had published, and should they accept this offer on my behalf. I immediately cabled that they should. It was very agreeable, this windfall of money for a story that had long since been sold and forgotten about. Others were sold later, and just before this present war I sold the British rights of twelve Sonny Tabor novelettes, all at one sweep. I've never seen any of my work as it was published in British magazines, and I often wonder how it was handled, and what was done, if anything, to change the dialogue so that it would be comprehensible to British readers.

I've often been asked about my writing methods. Every craftsman has his own peculiar way of doing things, and no two pulp writers that I have known go about their work in the same way. When writing a novelette I begin with the ghost of an idea . . . perhaps I think of a good title first, and the title suggests the story—then play around with an incident or two until it has grown and expanded into a story. All this without putting a word on paper. Perhaps several days elapse before the story has been mentally composed; sometimes this thinking-out process takes longer than the actual writing. Finally, however, I have enough to begin on, and on a single sheet of paper I sketch out the six or more chapters in a kind of bastard shorthand that no one but myself can read. Here's a sample, and not even its author can make head or tail of it now:

Gun Smoke on No Man's Range
Chapter i: Doc rides wild bronc, fixes man with toothache, gets acquainted with Cotton, is to call on Cotton's sick father.
Chapter ii: McRoss not sick, Doc refuses to consider mixing in range affairs, until he meets girl. Tell of Doc's father's ranch.
Chapter iii: Doc visits ranch, Northcott and men there; they order him to vamoose, and to leave town too.

Chapter IV: Cotton kills gunman, is arrested. Lynching threatened. Doc sees girl with Northcott, sees red.

Chapter V: Pretended smallpox scares off the lynchers, as Doc puts makeup on prisoner at jail.

Chapter VI: Doc's testimony at inquest, bullet's position in dead man shows not as gang claim. Cotton freed.

Chapter VII: Northcott man calls at Doc's office to kill him. Trick gunplay; he kills Northcott man instead. Rides.

Chapter VIII: They take shelter in ranch house, fight begins.

Chapter IX: Operation saves Northcott after Cotton's mother's plea. Girl explains. Doc gets her.

The above gibberish is all I need to start writing—in a short story I don't even use so much; the outline's purpose being to keep the chapters evenly balanced. Near the bottom of the sheet I write the names of the characters, one column of "bad men," another one of "sympathetic characters" and incidental names. These I select with some care, coining some and making others up from the telephone directory, using different first names to go with sometimes scrambled surnames. I think names are important, as some just naturally sound villainous, while others are vigorous and pleasing enough for the good men of the piece.

There was some love interest in the story I have used for an example, but most of them had little or none, and of course I could never marry off my series characters. That would have ended their careers with as much finality as having them killed.

I composed the stories directly on the typewriter, and fairly rapidly, writing it down just as it was to appear in the magazine. There was no other draft, and I do not revise or make changes after the story is written. A pulp writer with a large output should, I think, get into the habit of putting it down right the first time. If he works with the thought of revision in his subconscious he is apt to become careless and get into the attitude of "this isn't quite right, but I can fix it up later." This is only my own working method, however, and might not be acceptable to others. Of course, when a writer is doing something that he feels is especially important, he should revise and possibly entirely rewrite his manuscript, preferably when it is "cold." DeLancey Ferguson, in his recent excellent book *Mark Twain: Man and Legend* (Chapter 13), shows how the original manuscript of *Huckleberry Finn* was thoroughly and ruthlessly revised, almost every change being for the better. A good rule would be to write the script as if you never intended making a change (if you could so persuade yourself) and then to put it away for a month. Revise it then as if it were the work of your worst enemy.[18]

I've owned many typewriters, and prefer the heavy, standard size to the portable kind. For the past six years I have used machines with electric shift and carriage return. Typing, the way I do it, is hard work.

CHAPTER 11

Tumbleweed in Arizona

13. Bisbee, Arizona, 1999. *Author photo.*

An author's first book, no matter how poor it may be, is a milestone in his life, and before leaving California I had the somewhat awe-inspiring experience of appearing in cloth covers—of course, I mean my writings; I hadn't gone naked, exactly, all this time. The book was *Kid Wolf of Texas* by Ward M. Stevens, neatly bound up in gold-lettered red cloth and bearing the Chelsea House imprint. This was a subsidiary of Street & Smith, which had bought the book rights of five Kid Wolf novelettes for $150 and slapped them together to form something which, in length anyhow, was a novel.

As the stories had no connection with each other, the effect was not very good, except to dyed-in-the-wool Kid Wolf fans. There were to be no royalties paid, but it seemed to be a start, and I was thrilled when a dozen or so of the volumes were shipped to me. The next year another book was published on the same terms, this one entitled *Wanted—Sonny Tabor.*

As California was getting tedious, we picked up and drove back to Arizona, this time to the higher north country, for both Mary and I were eager to see snow again and feel the sting of frost. In Flagstaff we found just what we wanted, and a beautiful mountain forestland besides, a great contrast to the deserts of the south. Yellow pine timber spiked the rugged country in all directions, and toward the northwest loomed the white-capped San Francisco peaks. In the east and north again were the Sunset Mountain lava fields, a most peculiar volcanic formation that included ice caves and "The Devil's Plowed Ground." The region provided me with the locale for many Sonny Tabor adventures, and we made many side trips to Winslow, Snowflake, Prescott, and the Grand Canyon. It was a good hunting country, but while I did buy a Colt .45 and practiced with it, I could not, in spite of the bloodthirstiness of my fiction, go on any deer-slaughtering expeditions. I had seen too many of the critters, close up.

Before passing on, I want to say that Flagstaff has more brains per hundred inhabitants than any city in Arizona. Not only is there a college in Flagstaff, but it is the home of the Lowell Observatory, which was famous even before its discovery of the planet Pluto.

The next spring, hankering for a dry climate again, we moved to Nogales, the most important of the Mexican border towns west of Texas. As far as alcohol was concerned, of course, it was anything but dry. There was a brewery across the line, and twenty or more saloons, the most important industry in those days of American Prohibition. Some of the best food in the West was served at the International Casino, a landmark that has since burned, and where venison and other Mexican game (and game fish from the Gulf of California) were served by the old restaurateur, Alexander Rossi. Mexican Nogales was some three times larger than the American town, and both were orderly despite the thirsty American tourist trade, quietly conservative. Tijuana, Baja California, I had found depraved and vicious, but even this town is now as decent as many on our side of the boundary. Our anti-liquor laws injured all the North Mexican settlements, and our Drunken Neighbor Policy will be hard to live down.

Mary and I had motored from Tucson to be married in Nogales two years before, and now our son was born here—in the army hospital at Camp Little. Then, in less than a year, when we had moved back to Tucson, our family was completed with a daughter. By this time I was able to keep two establishments going, and in addition to the Tucson house I rented a shack in Madera Canyon where I did most of my writing. Madera was high enough in the mountains to be a relief after the blaze of the desert, and it was possible to tramp in comfort even in midsummer.

I remember one of these jaunts particularly well: first, because a rattlesnake struck at me, and in spite of the dread of heights that I was developing (I had once done a deal of mountain climbing, with great enjoyment, in my Colorado days) I almost jumped over a cliff in my haste to move from the vicinity; second, because of my companion, who grabbed me just in time. He was an interesting man, a little older than I, and a professional musician from Denver, a cellist who had been with a symphony orchestra. His young wife had developed tuberculosis, and they were making a brave fight against it together, a battle that, regret to say, was eventually lost. They had arrived in Tucson with very little money, and he told me a melancholy little story of the difficulty he had had, at first, of making ends meet.

"I put an ad in the *Citizen* soliciting pupils for the violoncello," he told me. "Our rent was past due, and we actually hadn't anything to eat in the house—the last half dollar had gone for the advertisement. I have a good instrument and I could have pawned it, I suppose, but with that gone I'd be as lost as you'd be without your typewriter. I've spent my life at music, and have no other way of making a living. So you see how desperate we were, especially after the day dragged along with no one making any inquires. Toward evening, just as we had begun to despair, a long limousine rolled up in front and a liveried chauffeur opened the door for a very haughty dowager and a little girl of twelve.

"It was a big moment. Yes, the woman was thinking of having her daughter taught the cello. They had come to Tucson for the winter, but had decided to stay at least a year, and the little girl could come for lessons three days each week. Somehow, I kept from fainting while terms were arranged. Money, of course, was no object, and substantial payments would be made in advance. She asked where I had studied and I was glad to be able to tell her I had spent two years in Europe. But still she hadn't made up her mind as to my competence; she sat tapping her foot and biting her lips thoughtfully. Suddenly she asked me to play for her.

"My wife took her place at the piano to play my accompaniment, first giving me a look that said 'Well, this is it.' The violoncello isn't the most effective of solo instruments, but I was determined to play as I'd never played before, nervous though I was. I gave my interpretation of some passages of Beethoven, then some Mozart. Looking at her out of the corner of my eye I thought she was still far from satisfied, and I set my teeth and played a very complicated and technical thing by another of the masters. The woman sat there through the whole thing, without moving so much as a diamond. After I'd finished there was a long, almost terrible hush. Then she asked me, 'That's nice, but can you play "My Blue Heaven?"'"

A book for writers, *This Fiction Business* by H. Bedford-Jones, came into my hands at about this time. Having a great admiration for Mr. Bedford-Jones's magazine work, I had bought the little volume on sight, and I didn't regret it. He had made a name in the pulps long before I had thought about writing, and few if any have published as much work. *This Fiction Business* was worth many times what I paid for it, for it gave me the courage to come right out and ask Ronald Oliphant for a raise in my word rate. Mr. Bedford-Jones coolly advised that hair-raising gamble when a writer was in a situation such as mine. Fully expecting a fearful bawling out, I wrote to Street & Smith with my request—and was immediately granted half a cent more. It sounds like little enough, but it amounted to a 50 percent increase. During the following years I was given additional raises without solicitation on my part. Once, when the depression was at its worst, and the banks had closed temporarily, I was asked to take a reduction, but this was returned to me within a few months.

The depression did not affect me very much, I am rather ashamed to say. People continued to read magazines—perhaps they were more in need of "escape" literature then than in better times. My depression was to come years later when the war had ended the unemployment problem for almost everyone—when my readers grew more prosperous, I grew poorer. Because of the paper and other shortages, the pulps at the moment are having a difficult time. So, in our different ways, are most of us.

After being helped by H. Bedford-Jones's pugnacious little book, I felt in his debt and have tried to repay it by helping other writers along, now and then—although I seldom go so far as to offer to read their manuscripts.

A young fellow who had made a sale or two, and who was anxious to make more, once called on me. He wanted to know how to break into *Wild West Weekly*. After telling him all I knew, I took him over to the home of a friend of mine, another writer who contributed to the magazine. My friend joined in the discussion of Street & Smith policies, but afterward he asked me if I thought we had done the right thing.

"He ought to have to dig it out the hard way, as we did," he complained. "When you tell him how to write for *Wild West* you're just making competition for us. I had a hell of a fight getting in there, and nobody made it easy for me."

"I had it pretty tough myself, but I know how that kid feels, Joe," I said. "And I don't think you need to worry about anyone crowding you out."

"I'm not so sure. And if you keep on, you'll have everybody writing Westerns and we'll be sucking the hind teat."

"I wish more good Westerns were being written," was my reply. "It would increase the public interest in our kind of story, and we'd be bound to cash in on it, even if others outshined us. First of all, the magazine we write for has to be a success, or you and I are out in the cold. I'd rather be sucking a hind teat, Joe—and get milk—than suck the best one, and have the cow go dry."

"All right, pardner," Joe said, "but just how many teats do you think our cow has got?"

Many writers think as Joe did, but I don't think a good workman in any profession needs to worry about his competitors—there's a mad, cutthroat scramble at the bottom of any of them, but that's because the novices keep their eyes on each other instead of on the target. The author who says that he is free of professional jealousy, however, is usually a liar. I feel pangs of it very often. It's good for me.

It can't be denied that the creative artist is sometimes a most peculiar goon. The other day I received a letter that reminded me of Dick Weaver, the Boy King of the Photoplay. It was from a detective-story writer, and following his name on the letterhead, which was decorated with skulls and revolvers, was the announcement that he was the author of more than thirty published books. Down the sides of the sheet and at the bottom were printed the list of his masterpieces, none of which I had ever heard of. The writer who advertises himself like that, I think, needs advertising.

Proud authors send you a copy of their book; but the really conceited one doesn't send you a copy—he thinks you've already read it.

Since Flagstaff, I had really begun to buy books, both for study and pleasure. I had always been a book lover, but after having had one of my own published I took a keener interest in the book itself, its physical form as well as the spiritual, so to speak. My symptoms of bibliomania became intensified as I gained a knowledge of modern authors and the first editions that represented them. What about first editions, anyhow? Why should a man in his right mind, presumably, pay hundreds of dollars, let us say, for a first issue of *Tom Sawyer* when he can buy a beautiful, well-illustrated modern copy of the same book for two or three dollars? Why should *Chance*, by Joseph Conrad, published in 1914, be worth from fifteen to twenty dollars, and copies of a later date fifty cents or a dollar? The 1914 *Chance* is only the second issue, too. The first issue, which is dated 1913, is worth many times twenty dollars. More recently, John Steinbeck's *Of Mice and Men* has what the collector calls a "point." The first issue is worth a premium because, near the bottom of page 9, the word "pendula" appears, and none of the later copies contains it. To the noncollector all this hairsplitting seems inane, but it's fascinating to the initiated. So much so that—but I'm not writing of book collecting. I will only say that I began to buy books, in a small way, and I still do buy what I can afford. I collect the authors who interest me, not trying for "completeness" in any; and I buy Western Americana whenever I can, along with anything else that takes my fancy.

Seldom do I buy or read Westerns. I once unconsciously "lifted" an episode and put it in my own work. This was at a time when I was only beginning to write, and I don't think I could unwittingly plagiarize now, but I have written so much Western stuff that it's a relief to read something as different from it as possible.

I had begun to realize now that the stories which were my livelihood were of no literary value; if not tripe, they were pretty close to it. The passing of my father, while I was in Nogales, had turned my thoughts toward philosophy, sometimes of the darkest kind; and since then I have done much heavy reading. The fiction I was writing had begun to dissatisfy me, and didn't come as spontaneously as formerly. The plan of a novel began taking shape in my mind, in spite of efforts to stifle it; then another book began crowding it. It was Dorothy Parker, I think (it *would* be Dorothy) who first spoke of being "big with book." Well, I was pregnant with two of them—twins—and both were tubal pregnancies, the out-of-place kind that cause so much grief to mother and child.

In the Kansas days, I had struggled to think of something to write a novel about; now I was being overwhelmed with novels that fairly screamed to be written. Still, I knew that I was still technically unable to handle them properly. The books are still unwritten. I didn't dare gamble, for I had others dependent upon my earnings, and the returns from a book are uncertain at best. It's true that I might have tried writing the more serious work in my extra time, but it my case it wouldn't have worked out. When a writer buckles down to his life work with the feeling that he must make full use of his talents or die, he can go in either of two directions: he can help to lighten the troubles of the world by bringing it laughter or entertainment; or he can write realistically, and put life down as his artistic eye might view it. Whichever path he takes, the writer won't go wrong if he gives the best that's in him. My trouble was, and is, that I wanted to be a realist, and a grimly fatalistic one at that. That kind of work simply would not mix in with the pulp fiction I was writing.

Edward S. Robinson, in his *Practical Psychology*, cited the case of a woman who developed skill both in fiction writing and in scientific investigation. But in order to write entertaining fiction she had to "forget herself and let fancy have free play—she must not be too critical." On the other hand, her scientific work seemed to require just the opposite frame of mind. She found these two systems interfering with each other. "The critical attitude from among her scientific habits was constantly interfering when she tried to write fiction or else was failing to appear with necessary vigor during scientific thinking . . . one of the two systems apparently had to be sacrificed if the other were to operate at maximum efficiency."[1]

And so I decided to postpone the heavy labor until a time when I was fairly sure I had the power to accomplish it successfully. I don't believe that a man is really ready to be a novelist until he is thirty-five. Forty is probably a better age at which to get really under way, and if the gods are kind to him and his cerebral arteries, he should have the best decade or two of his mental life ahead of him at that time.

In the meantime, although Kid Wolf, Sonny Tabor, and company were beginning to bore me, there were compensations. I could study life and books, and prepare myself for that fortieth milepost where, Mr. Pitkin says, life begins. And the wild cowboy stuff I was writing did, I think, bring more pleasure than harm to my fellow beings. For a long time, an old gentleman in South Carolina kept writing to me about Sonny Tabor, as though that brash young outlaw were a real person. Other correspondents did what they could to keep interested in Kid Wolf and John Socrates Forty-five. One day in Tucson an acquaintance took me to see his father, who was a watchman at a mining property some miles from town. The old fellow's shack was stacked with *Wild West Weeklies*, exclusively. Before he knew who I was, he told me how much he liked those "Ward Stevens stories." I was as pleased as Punch, as W. Somerset Maugham would say (is there a single story, by the way, in which Maugham didn't use that expression? Which shows that even the great have their pet clichés). Anyhow, it was such things as those that prevented me from becoming too weary of pulp writing. To that one man I was a great writer. Who could ask for more? But of course the writer does—he wants to multiply the man by millions.

And then, I'm disturbed by the thought that in all likelihood the man was a little crazy.

Among the writers I met who wrote for *Wild West Weekly* at one time or another were Bill Bruner, who wrote a long series of stories about "Vincente the Yaqui"; Chuck (Charles M.) Martin; and Lee Bond, creator of "The Oklahoma Kid." William F. Bragg and Walker Tompkins were among those I wanted to meet, but somehow didn't. Finally, after he had become a lieutenant commander in the navy, Allan R. Bosworth and I made contact by correspondence. Not content with *Wild West*, he began sending his yarns to the slicks, and a Western novel of his was serialized in the *Saturday Evening Post* not long before he entered active service.

From Tucson we trekked to the copper town, Bisbee, taking residence in the suburb of Warren. Over the Mule Mountains from there was the old town of Tombstone, rich in Western history. I visited it many times, retracing the adventures of the Earps, Ringo, and Curly Bill. The O.K. Corral, where the Earps and Doc Holliday shot it out with the Clanton bunch, is pretty much as it was when the guns were roaring. As the main road sweeps past the Bird Cage theater, through the town, and around past the Boot Hill graveyard, Tombstone is probably the best known of all the old mining camps.

Bisbee is a spectacular little city. It reminded me a little of Central City in the way that most of it teetered precariously on steep mountainsides, but Bisbee was far from being a ghost town, even though it was having its leanest days during my stay there. Its life depends on copper, which then wasn't worth the digging, but it was carrying on bravely with its chin up.

I'm afraid that my doings around Bisbee gave me a sinister reputation there. I believed then, and still do with reservations, that the more a writer knows of life, the dark holes as well as its bright pinnacles, the better equipped for his trade he will be—and for the same reason that I read a great deal of medicine and abnormal psychology, I investigated some of the more poisonous border fauna. My own curiosity and recklessness was quite a help. I managed to become friends with the Chinese colony in Naco. I liked those Chinamen—I was a bit suspicious of them at first, just as I had been of Mexicans, but all that is needed for a better feeling between races is a little understanding. I learned to play fan-tan with the Chinese of Naco, and on one occasion I smoked opium with them, although I don't want to give the impression that most of them used it. Or that I do.

In order to smoke, I had to be taken down into a cellar beneath a cellar—the stories about the Chinaman's fondness for underground passages are true; I believe he digs them for the fun of it. But then, narcotics are as illegal in Mexico as here, and my hosts had to use discretion. Anyhow, after I had stretched myself out on a straw mat, a Chinaman brought down a "layout" consisting of a pipe, an alcohol lamp, and several long skewers resembling hatpins. The opium was a sticky, tarlike gum contained in an old cold-cream jar, and along with the other narcotics of the opium complex it held morphine to a strength of about 10 or 12 percent. My squatting "cooker" now picked up a small lump of opium on the end of a long pin and roasted it over the lamp flame, rolling it often around the flat pipe bowl to shape it into a pill. When the little button of opium was cooked, and had changed to a light-brown color, it was quickly inserted into the tiny opening in the pipe. Then I was told to invert the pipe over the flame and inhale deeply (one who is not accustomed to inhaling tobacco smoke might find some difficulty at this point, but opium smoke "goes down" much easier even than that of cigarettes). After four or five long inhalations, the pill is consumed, and meanwhile your assistant has been preparing another one. After three or four pipes, I began to feel a languor in my limbs, especially the thigh muscles, and a not unpleasant constriction at the pit of the stomach. I didn't dream or lose consciousness—the only mental effect was the smoothing out of the bumps in the past, present, and future, and the feeling that I didn't give a damn about anything. Later, there was vomiting of a cerebral type and without much nausea. Of course, such experimenting has its dangers, but it isn't as easy to acquire the opium habit as most people think. Narcotics will never make serious inroads on the American people, simply because most people are normal, and normal people want to feel normal. With narcotics, you don't.

Cocaine is a much more vicious drug than any opium alkaloid, and the brain and nervous system deteriorate more rapidly under its influence. Although the habit is easier to break than those of morphine and heroin, the addict is likely to go back to it. It is especially dangerous for the adolescent, and that holds true for all drugs. The adult is not apt to inaugurate a craving, even after experimentation, but the youth of teen age is more susceptible because of awakening gland activity; at this time of his life he is rather erratic anyhow.

Federal laws—the Harrison Narcotics Act of 1915—cover only opium and coca, and their derivatives, and do not apply (or did not until recently) to marijuana, which is a weed that grows so commonly in the Southwest that the states find it difficult to control. It's simply an American variety of *cannabis indica (cannabis Americana)*—it's the hemp plant similar to the hashish of the Far East. Because its effects are somewhat between those of opium and those of cocaine, and because it is so easy to use, this plant is more menacing at present than any other poison. The marijuana weed is usually mixed with tobacco and rolled in a cigarette paper (corn husks are sometimes used in Mexico). The smoker takes long and rapid inhalations, but no effect whatever is felt for some time afterward, sometimes as much as a half or three quarters of an hour. Then the drug takes hold quite suddenly; the experimenter feels irresistibly compelled to laugh and does so uncontrollably even though his sensations are more unpleasant than otherwise. Marijuana is a deliriant, and it distorts the time sense so that the walking of half a block seems to require years, even centuries. It's for this reason that the weed has been used by a few musicians of the nightclub variety, one of whom told me that marijuana enabled him to improvise brilliantly. I have a fair ear for music, even for the modern popular sort, and this man's improvisations weren't nearly as good as he imagined they were. Because of the severe penalties attached to its possession and sale, it sometimes brings high prices in California, but personally I wouldn't give ten cents a ton for the weed. The swing band musician can have it, and welcome; a writer has a hard enough time staying sane without saddling himself with the reefer habit.

While on the subject of vice, I might add that Mexico takes a realistic view of prostitution. The government does not encourage the evil, but it doesn't shut its eyes to it; the women are segregated, and receive medical examinations which are regular and thorough enough to hold venereal disease to a minimum. In an establishment below the border, the entrance of which resembled an ordinary cantina, with a long bar and many bottles, I saw an official typewritten list of the inmates tacked just inside the door. As a former member of a Methodist Sunday School, I was a little shocked to see three names written at the bottom, with the notation that these employees were, alas, menstruating at the time and not available. In Mexico, as I pointed out, these things are regarded without prudery. But they do carry it rather far sometimes. "Indudablemente"—as my old Colorado friend of the pigeons would have said had he been a Mexican.

Bisbee has a hot summer climate, and to escape it we rented a cabin at Cave Creek, in the Chiricahua Mountains (pronounced approximately "Cheery Cow"). In order to reach it we had to drive through the Sulphur Springs Valley through Douglas and north for many miles to Rodeo, on the New Mexican side of the line, and then angle west again to the tiny settlement of Portal. The Chiricahuas had been my first glimpse of the Arizona I was approaching, some years before, and I'll never forget the grandeur of the spectacle when, south of Lordsburg, the great barrier comes into view across the valley. It rises abruptly, seemingly without foothills, to eleven thousand feet. Not far from here are the towns of Willcox and Bowie, and the famed Apache Pass. The history of this region was written in smoke and blood, for Cochise County was the last stronghold of the Chiricahua Apaches, probably the fiercest and most resourceful of all the Indian tribes. It was a peacefully beautiful country now, abounding with game. I often had to swerve the car to avoid striking deer. Cave Creek Canyon took its name from the numerous caverns that have been carved in its high, red walls.

Lee Bond and family came over from Tucson to spend some time up there. He and I poked our way into one of the largest of the caves, reaching it with some difficulty, at least on my part. We found the floor composed of the guano of birds and bats, the droppings of centuries. It stank considerably.

"My fortune's made," I jubilated. "I'm going to change my business and go in for fertilizer."

"What business do you think you're in now?" the Oklahoma Kid asked unkindly.

CHAPTER 12
Pilgrim in Santa Fe

14. Mary Powers, ca. 1931. *Collection of Patricia Binkley.*

Returning to California, I spent the next two years grinding out novelettes for the hungry maw of *Wild West Weekly*. I couldn't make any changes in my story formulas; the readers seemed to want my characters just as they were, and I must admit that Oliphant was right in saying that it was quite a job thinking up new adventures for my wild and woolly outfit of chivalrous gunslingers. When the repeal of Prohibition had come along, my editor relaxed the rules to the extent that my heroes might take drink, although of course they mustn't overdo it. This was a relief, for my he-men sometimes had quite a lot of business to do around barrooms, and their teetotalism had often embarrassed both themselves and their author.

We wanted to have a better and longer look at New Mexico, and because the northern half of that state would be new to us, we decided upon Santa Fe, sight unseen. Winter wasn't far off, and it was time the children were seeing snow. Sister Nell and her husband agreed to drive the car so that we could enjoy the strange luxury of a trip by train.

It's a peculiar thing, but you can't ride into Santa Fe on the railroad that bears its name. You have to pile off the train at a whistle stop, called Lamy, after the churchman Willa Cather wrote about in *Death Comes for the Archbishop*. Then you get onto a bus and ride for miles through the mountainous piñon country until, quite suddenly, there's Santa Fe in a crowd of trees, with the warm brown rock of St. Francis cathedral dominating the little valley. The altitude is seven thousand feet, and in the clear atmosphere the town stands out sharp and clean. It seems strange to you that this, the oldest of the state capitals, should have the most foreign flavor, and when you come into the plaza where the covered wagons were once drawn up under the trees you're glad, forthwith, that the railroad doesn't come here.

We were lucky to get a house, for it was still summer. In Tucson, the newcomer finds houses scarce and expensive in winter, but can rent cheaply enough during the hot months. In Santa Fe it is reversed, although it is more of an all-year-round resort than the Arizona city. The time to get located is when the summer crowd is leaving. After waiting a couple of weeks, we managed to rent at a very moderate outlay, a two-story "pueblo" on Canyon Road. You entered it through a high-walled patio where there was a fireplace for barbecuing; and there was a fireplace in every one of the *vega*-ceilinged rooms—and a thermostat-controlled furnace, just to make sure. The magnificent furniture was all handmade and very heavy, and on one of the balconies that overlooked the huge downstairs living room was the den and library, the books of which included the latest *Encyclopedia Britannica*. Once it had overcome its stage fright, my typewriter was very contented there.

The *Santa Fe New Mexican* announced my arrival: "Paul S. Powers, pulp writer, is occupying the Brooks house on Canyon Road . . ."

There I was, pigeon-holed and classified. For the first time, I was living in a community where a sharp distinction was made, socially, between pulp writers and—well, writers who amounted to something, writers who "counted." It was snobbery, we thought. Not that the really important authors of Santa Fe (the poet Witter Bynner, or Ernest Thompson-Seton, for example) were pompous or arrogant; they were not. It was the "arty" crowd of unsuccessful "would-be's" and the hangers-on that irritated me. In Tex Austin's bar one day I was patronized by one of these glib persons. He had almost had an acceptance from *Esquire* and was "dickering" with that magazine over another script that needed fixing up a little.

"You'll probably break into the slicks sometime yourself, Powers," he condescended.

I enjoyed telling him, "I was in the slicks quite a while, but after a lot of hard work I was finally able to break into the pulps."

He started to move away, then remembered just in time that I was buying the drinks. I know his kind pretty well. Many of those who jeer the loudest at the pulp magazines would sell their souls for a pulp writer's income. They've tried to write for the pulps, and failed.

While in Santa Fe I traded my car in on a new one, and the next day I came out of the house to see a wiry Spanish American youth polishing the automobile with a soft rag.

"My name is Pedro Bustamente," he said gravely. "I want the job of driving this car."

"I do my own driving," I stalled. "I can't afford a chauffeur. But thanks, just the same."

"I'll drive free. You don't need to pay me anything. I'm a good driver, too."

He was. To show me, he drove the car into the garage for me. Canyon Road was very narrow at that point, and as there was considerable traffic, I had found it difficult to swing the long car into its narrow stall at the very edge of the pavement. But Pedro Bustamente *backed* it in with perfect ease. I couldn't get rid of him, and soon I didn't want to. He hung around every day, trying to make himself useful, and he always had one eye on the greatly admired car. Pedro was a speed demon, but I learned to trust his driving, day or night.

He was at the wheel one afternoon when he asked if he might drive around to see "his family." We stopped at a little adobe at the edge of town where five or six children were playing. When he returned to the car, I asked about the small, heavy-set woman who had greeted him affectionately.

"Was that your mother, Pedro?"

"Oh no! She's my wife, and those kids they're mine," said Pedro, who must have been older than the twenty years he looked to be. "Twins the first time. My wife, she was in a hurry."

Later in the year I consented to lend him the car so that he could take his family down to Albuquerque for some sort of fiesta. When he came back he nonchalantly informed me that "one of the kids, not my kid but a friend of mine's kid, she got the back door open and she fell out of the car."

"Good Lord! Was the car moving?"

"Lucky I was only going fifty miles an hour. I happened to see the kid in the back-view mirror, away back there."

I had visions of investigations, lawsuits, and other horrors. "How bad was she—"

Pedro Bustamente shrugged. "Oh, she wasn't hurt any. I backed the car and picked her up. She's only three years old or I would have slapped the hell out of her to teach her not to fool around with those doors."

He was powerful, Bustamente was, and a fighter. Not only was he my chauffeur, but he had taken it upon himself to be my bodyguard as well. One night we entered one of the more disreputable saloons on San Francisco Street and were immediately set upon by two belligerent drunks. Pedro picked up the nearer one bodily and carried him out into the back room, although he was several sizes bigger than my driver, and I could hear the swift staccato of blows. Then Pedro reappeared alone, brushing off his hands.

"That damn dirty Mexican!" Pedro said. "Look out, Pablo!"

I had forgotten the other drunk until I heard Pedro's warning, and saw a fist swinging in my direction. It belonged to a tall, coppery-faced hombre who had a crazy look in his eyes. Instinctively I held him back with a straight left, and he sat down, unhurt but much intoxicated. Pedro picked him up and threw this one out the front door.

"Now put that bottle of Canadian Club on the bar," he told the bartender. "Keep your money in your pocket, Pablo. That tall one was an Indian. It's against the law to give liquor to an Indian. So we're going to drink free."

Bustamente was tough, and he had nerve. "Now that your wife is out of the room," he said one evening, "I can take my pants down. What you think of this, eh?" he asked, showing me a ragged six-inch scar on the lower right quadrant of his abdomen.

"Were you in a knife fight?"

Pedro shook his head. "No, I did this myself. It's where I operated on myself for my appendix. I did it three years ago when I lived at Socorro."

"Do you expect me to believe that, Pedro?" I laughed, for although I had read of a man performing an appendectomy upon himself, the patient-operator had been a surgeon and had done the operation in a hospital, under a local anesthetic. Even in that case, I suppose the surgeon had assistants to hand him the necessary tools, and of course all had been done with all the asepsis of modern science.

"I cut out my appendix," Pedro said earnestly. "I knew when it got to hurting so bad it was what my uncle had wrong with him when the *medico* cut his appendix out and charged him one hundred and fifty dollars dollars for. Why should I pay one hundred and fifty dollars for something I could do myself? Besides, I haven't got one hundred and fifty dollars, so when I can't stand it anymore I sharpen my knife and put it in boiling water. I also put in a big needle, and some thin fishing line, and boil it to kill all the germs. I shave my stomach and wash my hands clean. Then I push the table in the kitchen against the wall and I climb onto it. A looking glass I lay on the table, propping it up against a loaf of bread that is there; this is so I can see what I am doing. Then I open myself right along here—because I know that is where my uncle's scar is."

"Didn't it hurt?" I asked, still skeptical.

"Sure she hurt but I am already hurting so that I don't care. She didn't bleed very much, but I kept wiping it away with a clean towel so that I could see. Under the skin there are some muscles that run and up down, and these I pulled apart to get at the belly lining. I cut this lining and under this is some fat, like in an animal's belly. When I pull this away with my fingers I see my guts. You know there is a hell of a lot of guts in there? I can feel where I am hurting; I don't have to see so good, and I pull out some of the small guts until I come to the big guts. On the end of this is hanging my appendix, and it is swelled up bigger than my thumb. I lean back against the wall to rest a minute, and then I tie some of the clean fish line right where the appendix joins on, this so there will be no bleeding after I cut it off. Next I cut it off, and stuff my guts in back the way they were; they are slick and they slide in easy. I am through now, so I sew myself up, and then I drink a whole quart of wine and get down off the table and go to bed, I stay in bed three to four days then I get up and I'm all right. A doctor charges you a hundred and fifty dollars for that. Not me, he doesn't."

"Was there anything in the papers about that, Pedro?" I demanded.

"Nobody knew about it but my people. Why should it be in the papers? I didn't die, did I?"

"That's why it should have been in the papers."

When we left Santa Fe, Pedro Bustamente was in jail, where he was being held on the minor charge of gambling. I had gone down to see if I could pay his fine and get him out, but Pedro refused to leave the bastille.

"The damn Mexican who is in here with me still has money and we are still playing cards," he said. "But you could bring me some tobacco and an extra blanket. The food here is very good."

My Kansas-born older son was with us now. After several unsuccessful tries he finally broke his leg, and our journey back to the farthest West was a little delayed. This time it was again all the way to California for us. We journeyed by way of Flagstaff, which had changed but little, and the Grand Canyon, which had changed not at all.

Laguna Beach was our next stopping place, and we remained for nearly a year, until I finally decided that writers' and artists' colonies were not conducive to hard work, at least as far as I was concerned. Friends were always dropping in with a bottle, or still worse, without one. The Laguna Beach crowd was not so pretentious as some of the Santa Fe cliques, although it was close enough to Los Angeles to attract its share of crackpots. The little town is becoming overcrowded now. On a hillside far above the sea is a huge white house above a white cliff wall. Its builder never saw it completed; the great house stares out across the Pacific as if waiting for the return of the romantic forty-year-old boy who built it: Richard Halliburton.

I remember one occasion when Halliburton's mysterious fate was being discussed (he drowned, presumably, on his way to America on a Chinese junk), and Slim Sumerville, most unassuming of the picture stars, said something about the futility of human ambitions in general. James P. Olson, author of Western novels, solemnly clinked the ice in his highball glass and agreed. It came out that Jimmy's secret ambition was to act for the movies; Slim's was to write a book. And it suddenly came to me that offstage, Slim looked as a writer is supposed to look, while Jimmy could easily have been taken for a movie comedian. They might have had something there, both of them.

The other fellow's job is always more glamorous than your own. And better paid, too, considering everything.

CHAPTER 13

A Pulp Writer's Problems

15. Two pulp writers having a conference: Lee Bond (*left*) and Paul. Date unknown. *Collection of Patricia Binkley.*

The Smith Brothers—not the cough-drop pair with the beards, but those of the publishing house of Street & Smith—had died at an advanced age within a few days of each other. This had happened while I was in Santa Fe, and at the time I wondered what effect, if any, this event might have on that corporation's policies. It was probably coincidental, but there was a change. When a writer ties himself to one publisher he becomes hypersensitive to variations of wind and temperature. I felt that some sort of shifts were forthcoming, and in less than a year they began to make themselves evident.

Before going on, I want to say that I have, or have had, no quarrel with Street & Smith; there is no better outfit of pulp publishers that I know of; and any criticisms that I make shall be frank and sincere. After all, I know only the writer's side of the business.

The Saalfield Publishing Company of Akron had bought the rights to several of my novelettes, and the stories were made up into little books for sale in the dime stores. I received fifty dollars each for the stories, which, of course, had been originally purchased (American serial magazine rights only) by Street & Smith. I could also look forward to the disposal of other rights—book, radio, and movie, for example. Then I received a copy of an agreement from Street & Smith, which, I was told, I could sign or not as I pleased. It provided that the publishers were to handle all rights to my work in the future through a new department that was being set up. I was to receive a fourth of all the proceeds. My end of 25 percent seemed rather small, but I signed the document, and afterward "All Rights" was typed on my checks instead of "Am. Ser.R." That was the end of my "on the side" income, which, although it had never amounted to much, had always been productive of hope. Street & Smith had put across several radio features, such as "The Shadow" and "Nick Carter," and I heard that my own Sonny Tabor was on the air on some network in the South, but it was probably only a tryout, as was Sonny's comic book appearances. I began to get a bit discouraged as to the future of my "characters" and began to wish that I had an agent working all-out on their behalf.

The company had offered to purchase the rights to my characters way back in my Flagstaff days, but I had been wise enough, for once, to keep Kid Wolf, Tabor, and the others as my own property. Somehow, the idea of having other writers handling my brainchildren had given me the creeps.

We were living in San Diego when I got the word that Ronald Oliphant was withdrawing from Street & Smith's editorial staff. I had known, of course, that I couldn't expect Oliphant's tenure to last forever, but we were in rapport, so to speak, and our working together had been so pleasant that the news came as a shock.

With the new editor, who had formerly been a subordinate of Oliphant's, I got along very well, but with the passing of the months I became uneasy. Rather against my wishes, I had given Tabor, my outlaw character, a "pardon" and then had made him an Arizona Ranger, finally an undercover man, and as I had feared, most of the readers liked him better as he had been originally. I was asked to make a change, too, in my old method of setting down Kid Wolf's speech in which I had reproduced his Southern accent. On the other hand, I was allowed to put something more forceful than "blast you!" in the mouths of my villains, and I was glad to be able to put some mild profanity in the stories now and then. When I was asked to give Sonny Tabor a "sweetheart," however, I began to have really serious doubts. I did bring a girl into the Tabor series, much to the disgust of many of his fans, and it took some humping on my part to keep poor Sonny out of this additional hot water. I couldn't marry the fellow off, and neither could I permit him to consummate his love in an unethical way—not in *Wild West!* I suffered as much as Sonny Tabor, I think, during those months.

Then came a shake-up, and more editors for *Wild West Weekly,* along with an announcement that the magazine had heavily overbought and would not be purchasing anything again for some months. The blow came without warning. If they had been overbuying, it hadn't been from me, for I had been having all I could do keeping the stories going in fast enough and the magazine had been continually demanding copy. I had been expecting payment for a story of mine—I owed some of it for rent—but this story was held for months, with only curt explanations that didn't explain. Street & Smith had slammed the door, and of course I wasn't the only regular contributor who suffered. Christmas came and went, while I twisted and turned in an effort to remedy my dark situation.

My collection of books had to be sold, and any collector knows what a wrench that is. Fortified with considerable alcohol, I watched my first editions, my rare Coopers, Pike's *Expedition,* the Jack London manuscript and firsts, all go for a fraction of what I had paid for them. I had collected because I loved books, not for an investment, but the experience was painful from either viewpoint. The accursed dealers wouldn't even drink with me until the sale was over—the buzzards wanted to keep clear heads; afterwards, they drank to celebrate. Other things had to go, too, before the four or five months of my travail were over, including what I thought were friendships. Such episodes are good for a man's soul (even if hard on his family's stomachs) and one finds out who his real friends are, and which of his relatives have all the time been hating him just a little. I really had no complaint on the last score, and finally the clouds began to lift.

But the experience had awakened me, and I did considerable raging—and thinking. "Why, not even a workhorse would be treated this way," I gloomed. "A farmer doesn't just turn a horse loose to shift for itself in the wintertime with the expectation of catching him up next spring when there's more work to do. What if the horse starves to death in the meantime? Does the farmer just say 'Oh hell, there's lots of horses'?"

I had given my best to one company for more than a decade, and in return for that loyalty I had expected more consideration. Business, of course, is business, even in publishing; but I believe that cold hardheadedness can be carried too far, and that it usually is. However, in the writing game, you have to learn to take it. I had been in it long enough to know that, right well.

Naturally I had kept writing during my enforced layoff, and had sent the stuff to an agent who advertises rather widely. I shall call him Otto Hugo.

The first thing Hugo did, after sending me a bunch of literature describing and illuminating himself, was to tell me quite frankly that my work wasn't much good, that Sonny Tabor was naive, Johnny Forty-five silly, and Kid Wolf downright incompetent. I didn't mind that so much, but then he began abusing Ronald Oliphant, who, he claimed, was a nitwit. "If he was any good, he'd still be editor," Mr. Hugo advised me. Now, he knew the new editor of *Wild West*, was going to have lunch with him that day. And the new editor was smart; he didn't like those series stories and was going to do away with them when the magazine resumed buying. Now, if I was to sell anything, I must slant my stuff a new way. Those stories I had sent him, terrible as they were, might be sold somewhere, anyway; he, Mr. Hugo, would try. But they had trite plots and weren't "mature" enough.

Hugo did sell all the Westerns I had sent him—for half

a cent per word, on publication. I had been getting more than two cents, and promptly upon acceptance, so naturally I wasn't greatly cheered. I wrote to Hugo, giving my opinion of publishers who carried on their business in that manner, and suggested that, if agents were less prone to furnish these companies with material, there might be some chance of cleaning up the racket. I heard no more from Mr. Hugo.

As I have said, and will say again, the "payment upon publication" arrangement is unfair to the writer. Not only does he wait many months for his money, but sometimes he doesn't get paid at all. When the magazine *Judge* blew up, it did so owing me about thirty dollars for material it had published *six years* before. When I was in Warren, Arizona, I received a notice from a legal firm to the effect that if I wanted to put in a claim on the defunct magazine I should appear in person on such and such a date, whereupon I might receive a certain number of cents on the dollar. As the train fare to New York was considerable, I decided to let it slide. "There ought to be a law." And the law ought to forbid any publisher (except book publishers, who must use an entirely different system) making use of any material until paid for. If the publisher hasn't capital to carry on his business on such a basis, let him wait until he does have it. When I hear arguments on the other side I always think of my thirty dollars.

I started off inauspiciously with the new editors of *Wild West.* They insisted on a short story, first of all. Novels and novelettes had been my special dish for years, but I managed to write what I thought was a fairish one. It was returned, posthaste: the first rejection from Street & Smith that I had suffered in a dozen years. My new bosses wanted to let me know that new bosses were now in charge. The word "nerts" was scribbled on the script, and I knew that I had humorists to deal with. Anyway, it seemed that my story had no plot, and my style was wrong and full of clichés.

They were right. However, I had been at my business long enough to know something about it, myself. My style was simple and straightforward, without startling tricks. My readers had told me that I was easy to read, and I wanted to stay that way. I had noticed that many writers for the Western pulps went through all sorts of verbal acrobatics in telling their stories; I simply tried to be myself, endeavoring to tell my yarn in as simple a way as possible. And I think I was able to work in the interest and excitement that the reader wanted. The readers who like highly involved plots read detective or mystery yarns rather than adventure. In Jack London's best short story, "To Build a Fire," there is no plot to speak of. The man simply doesn't succeed in building the fire and he freezes to death. The story is all in the telling.

I said in the beginning that it is possible to write too well for the pulps. Walter van Tilburg Clark's powerful Western *The Ox-Bow Incident* would have been rejected by any wood-pulp magazine editor, and I think most of them would have returned it with only a rejection slip for comment. A few might have taken the trouble to write to the author: "Sorry; not for us; over our audience's heads; try Sat. Eve. Post." But in any event the pulp editor would be quite right in returning it. Their readers wouldn't have liked that splendid story. They don't want to think; they want to be entertained. They know what they want and they insist on getting it.

What worried me was my suspicion that the new editors were trying to turn *Wild West Weekly* into something like the run-of-the-mill Westerns that were crowding all the newsstands. I hoped that the magazine would be kept "wild" and that I wouldn't have to send my characters around on motorcycles. It had an unique flavor, and I thought, and still think, that there will always be a place for it.

The reader is, after all is said, the final arbiter, and I'm glad to be able to say that mine didn't let me down. Wolf, Tabor, and company were as popular as ever, and soon they were in full swing again, with *Wild West* sending me frequent calls for more and more work. One of the first things I did was kick Sonny Tabor's sweetheart out of his stories, and I finally arranged it so that he could become a "wanted" man and a fugitive from justice once more. Rather tough on Tabor, but that was the way his fans wanted him. I also brought back King Kolt, who hadn't appeared for some time, and evolved a new set of characters called "The Fighting Three" just to see if I could still do it. They were not startlingly original, of course, but the *Wild West* addicts seemed to like them.

Before leaving the subject, I want to say that my experience with Otto Hugo doesn't mean I'm down on agents. Far from it. A writer needs such help, especially the one who is just established enough to feel that his work is all salable *somewhere;* it's the agent's business to know *where,* and he is in a better position to understand markets than the writer himself.

Many writers swear by Otto Hugo. It just so happened that he used the wrong method in handling me and that our personalities clashed. I'm like many others in that I respond to praise rather than abuse; I'm a bit touchy, and my complexes are easily pushed over to the inferiority side. Nagging might stimulate some, but I know that I'm at least as good a workman as the average, and I don't mind being told so. And why was Otto Hugo down on Ronald Oliphant? I think it was because Hugo had, for a long time, been trying to squeeze *his* stable of writers into *Wild West* and that he resented the space that was given to me. Such is politics in the pulp industry. Oliphant was very competent, and the magazine made money under his direction. An astute company such as his doesn't publish a magazine every week for a dozen years just for the fun of it.

All this, of course, will interest professionals only. I hope I've been able to avoid talking too tediously of shop in this now nearly finished book. But I would like to say something about social security for writers.

I believe the present system of insurance against want should be extended to include all the professions. In order to succeed at his work, the author must be a pretty rugged individualist, but he has the same tendency to become old as anyone else, and through unfortunate investments or otherwise he is sometimes badly in need of help that he is too proud to ask for. I've heard all the sneers against "paternalism" and most of the threadbare arguments that have been presented by people who, for all they know, might need security sometime themselves. The brain worker, the freelance writer, the artist, the dentist, all the "self-employed" should be required to insure themselves with the government against age and misfortune. I've known once brilliant and successful doctors who have died in friendless poverty—some have drifted out here to the West in order to do it. The war and its aftermath might teach some of these "rugged" independent folk who jeer at social betterment that unless we achieve "freedom from want" we may soon be facing "want of freedom." Why all this preachment? Because I can't get the case of Eugene Manlove Rhodes out of my mind. In his biography, *Hired Man on Horseback*, it is poignantly told how his last days were spent in an agony of financial worry; there was no money for postage, hardly enough in the house to eat. All this in San Diego where I was living at the time! Nobody knew, of course. Gene was the best Western writer of them all. I shall never forget reading his "Under, Over, Around or Through" in the *Saturday Evening Post* when I was in my early teens. His books are now much sought after by collectors, for his stories will live. Toward the last, the *Post* rejected some of his, ironically enough. He was old and tired, and everyone, when they knew afterward, was a little bit ashamed of America. Except those who said, "Well, why didn't he save his money?" There is no shame in them.

The future of the pulps? I believe they will come back stronger than ever after the war. Many have been suspended for the duration in spite of their popularity in the armed services. One of the things that I hope will come with peace is a stronger organization of the professional writers of this country. When it comes I'll join with enthusiasm.

The discipline of the war has been good for us all. Personally, I hope that the pulp-writing phase of my life is about finished, and that I will be ready for the serious work that every author feels that he *must* write. My jolting of two years ago showed me the depth of the rut I was digging for myself; one can't really estimate such a thing until he begins to crawl out of it. A chance to write my best is all that I ask of life now. I've learned the unimportance of luxuries, of "cars bigger than the Joneses' car," and other foolishment. I would like to write enough books so that I could buy books enough.

Meantime, there's the war. It's taken me time to get things all arranged, but before this book is published I expect to be in navy uniform, to join my elder son, who, as a pharmacist's mate is fighting in the far Pacific.

The End

Life after the Pulps

16. Paul, Pat, and Tom, ca. 1948. *Collection of Patricia Binkley.*

I n October 2001, two years after we first met and sorted
through Grandpa's papers, my aunt Pat called me. She
had found another journal. With this journal and the
other documents in the original collection, I was able to
piece together what happened to Grandpa after the end of
the pulps and the publication of *Doc Dillahay*.

By 1938, Street & Smith was a ghost of its former self. Titles
such as *The Shadow* still sold, but the Western magazines that
had carried the company from its beginning were struggling.
Readers' tastes were changing, but Street & Smith stubbornly
clung to their Victorian story lines, and *Wild West Weekly* and
Western Story Magazine doggedly pursued a West encapsulated
within a mythical frontier. Competing magazines such as
Dime Western and *Big-Book Western* featured realistic and gritty
heroes in stories lined in gray, but Street & Smith clung to
characters who were pure and unquestioning in their pursuit
of evil. Good was good and bad was bad.

Grandpa asked for an advance of four hundred dollars
in March 1938. Why he needed the money is not clear, but
judging from Oliphant's comment in the letter accompanying the money, the root of the problem was probably physical. Grandpa suffered from what he called "polyneuritis" in
his hands, probably caused by ten years of pounding on a
typewriter, and it undoubtedly affected his production. But
Oliphant didn't let sympathy cloud his management of the
magazine. The very next letter, fifteen days later, consisted
of two questions: What was the status of Grandpa's writing
progress, and where was the next Kid Wolf story?

That same year, Street & Smith overhauled management. For the first time in its history, the company was run by people outside the family. Anyone who didn't fit into the new plan was promptly fired. One of the casualties was Ronald Oliphant. Transitions are always hard, but Oliphant's absence of was especially difficult for my grandfather, who missed the editor's fair and gentlemanly approach, especially when it came to Grandpa's recurring tardiness when turning in stories.

Grandpa doesn't mention his constant struggles to meet *Wild West Weekly*'s deadlines in his memoir. From about 1932 on, he frequently turned in his stories late, or sometimes he just disappeared for a month or two. As the following letter indicates, his lapses occasionally resulted in considerable backloads:

September 6, 1934

Dear Powers:

Since you've been in San Diego you seem to be slipping rather badly on production. Why not go back to that nice canyon in Arizona where you used to do so much work?

Will you please make your next job a short novelette about Sonny Tabor (12,000 words) with a Thanksgiving setting suitable for the Thanksgiving number? I should also like to have some Kid Wolf and Sonny Tabor novelettes of 15,000 words suitable for cover illustration and shorter novelettes about both characters of 12,000 words, as well as independent novelettes and an occasional yarn about Freckles Malone and Johnny Forty-five.[1]

Francis L. Stebbins, an assistant editor who wrote many of the Bar U Twins stories, took over the lead for *Wild West*

Weekly after Oliphant left. Grandpa dutifully turned in stories that were, for the most part, stale and tired. Judging from Stebbins's letters, Grandpa was utterly exhausted. Stebbins gently chastised him, warning him to stay away from the old plots and clichéd characters. But Grandpa, crippled by mental block or burnout, could not produce. Stebbins, who by this time was affectionately signing his letters "Steb," sent Grandpa two- and three-page letters with detailed, involved story outlines to use.

Grandpa asked for an advance again in 1940, but this time he was turned down. "The only thing I can suggest," answered Stebbins, "is that you bear down plenty hard on the writing, even if it doesn't come easy under financial worries, and keep shooting stuff along pronto prontito. . . . These are evil times for pulp writers and editors both," he continued. "The 'good old days' are gone."[2]

But the heroes in *Wild West Weekly* were still entertaining their readers, and they were doing it well. Blacky Solone, created by James P. Webb, was a popular hero in 1941. Blacky had started out as a Texas Ranger, but he was impatient in trying to get information from suspects and roughed them up a little too much, which didn't sit well with his father, Ranger Captain Jack Solone. Blacky was reprimanded, but chafing under authority, the strapping young "trouble hunter" with black curly hair and a easy grin deserted. He went on his way, looking for outlaws to capture, using his Texas Ranger badge when he thought fit. Blacky was a "Dirty Harry" of sorts, as can be seen by the following passage from "Pilgrim on the Prod":

"I've done told the sheriff," the foreman grunted. "I ain't tellin' you anything."

Blacky chuckled; his black eyes brightened with amusement; he made two slow steps forward.

Then with a suddenness of a lightning flash, he

swarmed over Borman, slammed him back against the wall, and fell on top of him. He twisted the foreman's right arm up between his shoulders in a hammerlock. Bowman yowled.

Blacky said casually, "Other people have made the mistake of thinkin' they wouldn't tell me anything, and it always makes me mad. Unless you answer my question, I'll break your arm this time."[3]

Señor Red Mask, created by Guy Maynard, had a triple identity: besides the Señor, he was really Tom Goodwin of the Bar G Ranch, but when need be he put on a sombrero and hoisted a guitar, calling himself El Muchacho and claiming to be a poor ranch hand. It was his way of gaining entrance into crowds who would have never allowed Señor Red Mask, crusader for the downtrodden, to enter. El Muchacho came, sang a few songs, gathered information he needed, and split.

A third editor appeared in 1941. John Burr, *Western Story Magazine*'s editor, was asked to add *Wild West Weekly* to his workload. Efficient Burr may have been; diplomatic he wasn't. No longer did Grandpa have the luxury of dealing with an editor like Oliphant who would never, even in tense moments, lose his gentlemanly composure. Although Burr began with faintly veiled missives such as wanting to know "*at once*" when a story would arrive, that didn't last. He quickly lost patience with Grandpa's habitual tardiness:

"According to your wire of July 14th, you say that Kid Wolf is due before August 1st. I'm very much upset inasmuch as I told you in my letter of July 17th that the copy should be here on Monday the 28th. Would you be good enough to reply at once and give me definite dates so that I know where I am? I cannot continue to work with you on such a nebulous basis."[4]

When Grandpa voiced his concerns over the magazine's future, Burr replied:

Of course you were late with Johnny Forty-five, and you said in your letter of the 13th that we would have a Kid Wolf "by air on Monday, the 16th." This is Wednesday, the 18th, and I see no sign of Kid Wolf. . . . As to your request for information about business—it strikes me rather screwy. We're doing all right here and are continuing to put out magazines. I think I have said once before that I'm not the Oracle of Delphi concerning when "will we run out of paper, money, or something." And all the assurance I can give you is that we will carry on and expect you to do the same.[5]

Burr's job was to "mature" *Wild West Weekly* by toning down the juvenile nature of the yarns. One of the first changes he made was to stop using the Western "singsong" language that had permeated the magazine since the beginning. "You" replaced "yuh," for one thing. In addition, Burr didn't care for the magazine's long-standing tradition of featuring several regular heroes. Suddenly, the issues occasionally appeared with only one hero: a Circle J story, an Oklahoma Kid, or a Kid Wolf would be a feature novel. All other stories in the issues would be "independent" stories that did not feature a regular *Wild West Weekly* hero.

The strategy backfired. Readers of *Wild West Weekly* bought the magazine for a reason: to enjoy heroes they could count on week after week to behave in a certain manner. They didn't need some citified editor telling them what to read. Letter after letter after letter to the editor complained of the new format.

Dear Range Boss:

I am writing in regard to your magazine. For the last year it has been rotten. Leave out the gals and the continued novels. Run the magazine the way it used to be.

Delbert Ganns[6]

Dear Range Boss:

I have been reading your magazine four years, and I think it is the best on the newsstands. Lately, however, you have been using too many new authors and characters. I wish you would go back to the old characters, such as Sonny Tabor, Oklahoma Kid, Tommy Rockford, Kid Wolf—instead of so many new ones.

Also, I would like to see you continue the Wrangler's Corner.

Adios,

Howard Lassen[7]

Even my father sent in letters, sometimes disguising himself as "Ward Stevens Jr." The following letter (written under his real name) appeared in the January 31, 1942, issue, after the magazine had reverted back to its old ways. I'm sure his father stood behind him with glee as he wrote this.

Dear Range Boss:

Congratulations!! It looks as if the old, sick 3w is gradually pulling out of the rut. Let's hope that we will soon be able to sit back in our favorite chairs and comfortably read a 144-page Wild West Weekly (price 15 cents), with rough edges on it to boot.

And as we readers relax and devour a Kid Wolf or Señor Red Mask yarn, we will chuckle when we look back at the disastrous years of '39 and '40, when the magazine was very, very sick—when it had smooth edges, girls in the stories, and continued novelettes. Let's hope it won't be long until that memory will be possible to experience.

I think I have a question which won't be answered, Range Boss—but can you ride a hoss? Can you shoot a .45, rope a steer, or stick on a sunfishin' bronc? Be honest now, Ed. Chances are that the only thing you've ridden is a swivel chair at 79 7th Avenue. But if you continue your swell work, us readin' hombres have no kick coming, have we?

... We all know that you editors ain't superhuman, but there's sure a lot to be done before 3w's rehabilitation will be complete. After all, we're the guys who push the dime across the counter.

Yours for a bigger, better, and et cetera, et cetera Wild West Weekly . . .

Jack Powers
(3w Club, Member No. 1.)[8]

Pulps circulation continued to sag. They were losing their novelty; the comic book had become enormously popular. The war was on, and many boys who had sat on their back porches reading *Wild West Weekly* were now fighting in the Pacific. What eventually killed the pulps was, ironically, the feature that made them unique in the first place: the paper on which they were printed. During World War II, all types of raw material, including steel, aluminum, nylon, and rubber, became property of the war effort. Since paper was another material in short supply, the entire newspaper and magazine industry was affected. Many pulp magazines quietly signed off.

Wild West Weekly hung on, sturdy as ever, but changes began to appear. The editors tried new a new look by changing the title logo. Once in a while a great artist like Walter Baumhofer created a gem, but many times the artwork was flat and uninspired. The early years, when the H. W. Scott covers exploded with action but, at the same time, were graced with originality and freshness, were gone. In 1943 the magazine cut back on its size and the frequency of publication. The publisher began using reprints for covers. Eventually the interior illustrations were taken from the *Western Story* and *Cowboy Stories* banks. With the March 13, 1943, issue, *Wild West Weekly* went from a weekly to a biweekly, its name shortened to *Wild West*. That September it was changed to a monthly.

But even up until the summer of 1943, Burr was continually asking for more production from Grandpa, even offering him two cents a word for the Fightin' Three fellows. Burr was in a good mood, saying, "more ups to come, so it's not such a dismal world after all."[9] He finished with jokingly offering Grandpa a heavier schedule than the one he had recently given him.

But the tone changed abruptly with a July 20 letter: "The check for 'Death Blots the Brands' left our office yesterday and will no doubt reach you before this letter. P.S. From now on all stories will be limited to 12,000 words."[10]

There was nothing particularly different about the November 1943 cover. It was like all the others: a cowboy on a pinto, forging a creek as the cowboy looks back at his pursuer. Grandpa had two stories in the issue, one of which the cover claimed was a "flaming" Johnny Forty-five story called "Hog Legs for Range Hogs." Johnny provides one of his famous four-liners:

> When your knees are rattlin' on the rope,
>   And your neck is stretched good and far,
> When you're squirmin' and twistin' and turnin'
>   Then you'll look like the snake that you are.[11]

The other was a Fightin' Three of the Rockin T story, "Death Blots the Brands." This series had a lot of promise for Grandpa. But inserted close to the end of the story was a caption: "Because of the drastic necessity for the conservation of paper and because we are doing everything in our power to co-operate with our government in winning this war, we announce, with regrets, that with this issue WILD WEST will suspend publication for the duration."[12] Although the notice insinuated that the magazine was only temporarily on hold, it would never be resurrected.

After the magazine shut down, Grandpa sporadically sold stories to big pulps that managed to stay in business, such as *Western Story Magazine, Thrilling Ranch Stories*, and *Ranch Romances*. Judging from the meager correspondence from *Western Story Magazine* in Grandpa's papers, the volume he produced for them was a fraction of what he had written for *Wild West Weekly*. Grandpa, almost forty years old, had to start all over again as an apprentice writer, struggling to write stories that might or might not get published and wondering how he would pay the rent.

Other *Wild West Weekly* writers also had mixed success after the magazine ended. Chuck Martin wrote to my grandfather in October 1949:

Dear Paul:

I received your letter as I was on my way to serve at City Hall on Public Relations Committee, and took time out to read it first. Feller, it's damn peculiar how many times History repeats herself almost identically in different individuals.

What you are going through now, I went through three years ago. I made the transition you did. I quit pulp. I conditioned (or air-conditioned) my mental attitude to do the better writing. Put over three books and hell, it takes 18 months from when you start, until you collect the first royalties. That eating in between is hell.

I did one book and quit. I returned to pulp for a stake, I just could NOT serve two masters, pulp and Literature. And I turned out damn poor pulp. My heart wasn't in it, like when you and Lee B and I were earning our cakes and pudding from 3w.

I quarreled with Editors, principally Leo Margulies. But I did sell the cheaper markets. By then I wasn't proud. I stopped thinking about how much a word, and started thinking about how much could I earn in a month. This thing you are going through now, hit damn near every old-timer in our contemporary group. It damn near killed Bob Bond. Who, by the way, left Laura and went to Okla. Got a dee-vorce, and I understand is now married again.

I wish to hell you could run down here for a day of this and that. Most of the other old-timers have been down; we've ironed out a lot of bugs on this INCOME thing, and how to get it. Tain't a NICE way, Paul. Not the way you or I would have earned our cakes ten years ago. But it IS . . . a LIVING. That's all I wanted.

I BLEED when I see some of my old trail-pards in this writing RACKET. Good guys of proved ability, you know; the slings and arrows of outrageous fortune. There's this about our breed, Paul. We stick together, help each other where we can, and God help the Johnny-Come-Lately who disparages one of the old MASTERS in our presence. . . .

The bright YOUNGSTERS were going to take our places. Well look Paul; they DID. Then they got big-headed. Were gonna write slicks. Now they are all starving. They never will again be good PULP writers. Down in your heart, and mine, we know damn well we are not ashamed of our pulp record. Some of your Sonny Tabors were classics. Some were lousy, just like some of my Rawhide Runyans. But the high percentage were good.[13]

Martin did adjust, however, catering to the paperback field. He had good advice for Grandpa, telling him to try to get his

Sonny Tabor stories reprinted, especially overseas. The juvenile market was strong. Martin was doing Western juvenile books himself for Viking Press. Grandpa wouldn't follow his advice, however. He was too busy writing *Doc Dillahay*.

Walker "Two-Gun" Tompkins had better luck. Someone who wrote six thousand words a day, five days a week wasn't going to just stop cold turkey. Tompkins ultimately wrote twenty-seven novels and scripts for various television shows. Later he wrote books of regional history for the Santa Barbara area. He died in 1990.

As for Ronald Oliphant, he settled down on Staten Island and wrote pulp stories, selling them to the new editor of 3w, Francis Stebbins, and a few to Leo Margulies, managing editor of Standard Magazines. He may have migrated west, presumably to be closer to his son Malcolm, who was born about the same time as Grandpa's children. Public records show Ronald Oliphant died in 1968 at the age of eighty-three in Signal Hill, a dozen or so miles from Grandpa's last residence in southern California.

The last pulps were discontinued in the late 1950s, although *Ranch Romances* held on until 1970. All in all, roughly twelve hundred pulp magazine titles came and went during their heyday.

In 1943, Grandpa, Mary, Tom, and Pat lived in a large home on tree-lined Grand Avenue in Orange, California. Orange was surrounded by orange groves, strawberry farms, and fruit orchards. Knotts Berry Farm, just down the road in Buena Park, was a berry stand and a fledgling chicken restaurant. The house on Grand wasn't far from downtown, but its expansive backyard and fruit and magnolia trees gave the house a country feel. It was the largest house for many blocks around.

Unfortunately, the pastoral setting wouldn't last. A few years after *Wild West Weekly* shuttered up, the family moved

17. Jack and his bride-to-be, Ruth Selton, ca. 1946. *Author's collection.*

to a smaller home on La Veta Street, the "hovel" that my
mother remembers.

But at least the kids were thriving. Tom and Pat attended
the local high school, playing tennis, having some semblance
of a normal life, finally. Jack entered the service and was
fighting in the Pacific. Grandpa never joined him, however,

as he suggests at the end of the memoir. He was almost forty at that point; he might have been too old to enlist.

Jack had grown into a spirited and athletic boy, tan and lean and with movie-star looks. He was only five foot seven, but he acted as if he soared above everyone else. In 1947 he married Ruth Selton, a pretty blond originally from Ohio and the only child born to Martin and Flora Selton. Grandpa's first grandchild, Linda, was born in September of that year, and Patricia, named after Jack's sister Pat, arrived eighteen months later. Jack was suddenly a younger image of what his father had been at twenty-two: a father saddled with responsibilities but still full of vigor and energy. He started medical school and worked on and off in various shoe stores to help pay the bills. He tipped the elbow once in a while just like the old man did, but it was nothing to be alarmed about.

Doc Dillahay was published in 1949. Reviewers across the country were charmed. The *New York Herald Tribune* called it "warm and vibrant, handling the stuff of melodrama in terms of character instead of the stock formulas of the badlands." The *Los Angeles Times* said: "This story of the 1800s has both the excitement of the old West and the substance of at least one phase of its expansive history, and perhaps that is why 'Doc Dillahay' is growing in popularity."[14] One of the few mixed reviews was from the *New York Times*, which said that the book was "almost plotless," but at the same time said it was "an interesting and very readable story." They especially loved the character Dr. Ledinger, whom they noted was a "lovable, gifted drunkard . . . a character to remember."[15]

It appeared as if financial relief was imminent. Grandpa was continuing to get envelopes from Macmillan that were full of clippings of pleasant reviews for *Doc Dillahay*. He didn't have any reason to believe that the money wouldn't soon follow.

But by the end of the year, Grandpa was getting more and more nervous about the royalty checks he was receiving. He was getting some checks, but it was the amounts that were the problem: $76.25, $81.65, $332.45. Certainly not a pittance, but not as much as he was expecting.

Macmillan approached Grandpa about doing a Dillahay series. Excited, in 1950 he started a sequel called *The Young Dillahays*. After a year of writing on his part and a great deal of anticipation on Macmillan's part, he sent the first few chapters to the publisher for their perusal. They were shortly returned with the following letter:

July 17, 1950

Dear Mr. Powers:

I certainly don't like to have to write you this letter, because I know how disappointed you are going to be when you hear that we don't see our way in making a contract for THE YOUNG DILLAHAYS on the basis of the sample chapters you have sent us. They are competently written, and I for one found them interesting, but others here feel that you are straying too far from the accepted western pattern, and that you are perhaps not on the right track in putting so much emphasis on the love story. There is no reason why there shouldn't be a love story, and a moving love story, in this book, but we don't want to lose sight of the western element, and it looks as though that was happening. After all, we are going to have to sell this book to western readers. . . .

Sincerely yours,
Eleanor Daniels[16]

Grandpa seems to have thrown up his hands over the project at that point, judging by the next letter he received from Macmillan:

October 13, 1950

Dear Mr. Powers

I have just now come back from my vacation, and I find

on my desk copies of the Bantam edition of DOC DILLA-HAY, now known as SIX-GUN DOCTOR (and a good title, don't you think?). I was glad, not only to see the reprint, but to be given an excuse to write, because I have been troubled about you and hoping that some word would come from you.

We are all most interested in your writing, and we don't want to think that you have abandoned a second book. Won't you let me know how you are making out? Naturally, our reaction to the sample chapters from THE YOUNG DILLAHAYS must have been hard to take, but I want to reiterate what I said in my last letter, that we have immense faith in you and that we know there will be another book by you, stronger and finer and, to get practical, even more saleable than DOC DILLAHAY.

I would certainly be glad to find a letter from you on my desk. In the meantime, four copies of SIX-GUN DOCTOR are on their way to you, and they will bring our very best wishes and the assurance of our continued interest in you as a Macmillan author.

Sincerely yours,
Eleanor Daniels
Associate Editor[17]

The sequel was never finished.

By the spring of 1951, Grandpa and Mary's living situation had worsened considerably. Grandpa had sold fewer and fewer stories to the remaining pulp magazines, and they had sunk deeper into debt. Jack and Tom, both of whom were in school in the Bay Area, had discussed with Grandpa and Mary their moving north to be closer. This seemed to be as good a time as any, Jack wrote; a change of scenery could help Grandpa get out of his writing funk. As he said, a change of scenery was always good.

18. Mary in one of the bookstores in Berkeley, ca. 1960s. *Author's collection.*

In March 1951, Grandpa and Mary were evicted from the house on La Veta Street. They packed up the remainder of their belongings and moved to Oakland, a move in stark contrast to their insouciant moves during the pulp years when they left personal belongings behind, confident that there would always be income to replace them. They rented a twelve-by-ten room from an elderly woman on Parker Avenue off College Avenue, not far from the Berkeley campus where Tom was a pre-med student.

Once they were settled into their new location, Grandpa began writing a journal. It opens on a somber note:

Evening . . . no attempt to be "literary" in this record, just the facts. Cash on hand tonight, 16 cents. We've been much lower since coming here. Yesterday we called Mt. Zion Hospital in SF (pay call) twice, to sell blood. Understand that we'd receive $24 each (Jack has given a number of times). Had to call at 3 sharp, did so . . . told that they weren't taking the names "yet"; called back in five minutes and were too late. "Call next week." By next week we probably won't have any blood.[18]

The entry, dated June 9, 1951, shows how precarious their situation had become. Grandpa's royalty checks for *Doc Dillahay* had all but stopped coming. Mary began to look for a job, but there wasn't much available for a middle-age woman with no work experience. The room they rented had only a hot plate with two burners for a kitchen. They had no radio, no television, not even a clock. At some point Jack lent them a radio, so at least they would be able to know the time of day. They lived on sardines and lima beans.

The entry for that date continues:

Isn't our luck bound to change? But when? I have taken no drink since leaving Orange, under a cloud of debt, and I suppose sneers. But I simply could not go on living there and remain still half sane. . . . But no alcohol for me here, no temptation to take any in spite of all these pressures (my fingers are crossed, but I think I have it whipped). The change of locale did me good; this is a more civilized place . . . if one had enough money to live comfortably it would be a paradise; for me, anyhow. Good books, art, music, theater . . . people you can talk to if you haven't forgotten how. We had less than $100 when Mary reached here (out of $500 that didn't go far down there in paying debts). Since then my income (!) has been about $77, from a story that the agent had sold months before. No sale since; I have four in (two pulps, two better ones, that the agent said he liked and hoped to place). Now I'm waiting for that MacM decision. If I could only get a green light, and maybe, in a few weeks, a $250 advance . . . heaven.

. . . Looking back over the years I wonder what's happened. What I wouldn't give to have those $800 months like I had writing the pulps.

But I had to pay for those "easy" years; how much longer must I pay? My ideals . . . wants . . . have changed, if it's not too late. Sometimes I think, no matter what the "circumstances" a man will be just so happy, no more, no less: for instance, I feel as elevated now over a rare find in a bookstore as I used to in a new car. And I don't have to go get drunk over the book. This hobby has saved me, so far . . . when we're absolutely broke I miss the long walks to Oakland or around Berkeley, more than the lack of groceries.[19]

This "hobby" was Grandpa's daily hunt for rare books. He was what book dealers called a "picker." Unlike book dealers who found most of their inventory from estate sales or major collectors, Grandpa went out every day and looked for books in the secondhand stores and then sold them to the bookstores in town. In Berkeley, as in all college towns, bookstores thrived. One could walk down any street within a few miles' radius of the campus, and a bookstore could be found on every other block. The town was also full of salvage shops and stores where students could buy secondhand clothes and furniture.

The setup was perfect for Grandpa, who could do it all on foot or, if need be, by bus. He walked around Berkeley or down to San Pablo Boulevard in Oakland and rummaged through the book bins at Goodwill, Vet's Salvage in Oakland, Volunteers of America Salvage, or Holmes' outdoor bins, where he'd find a copy of *Tricolored Sketches in Paris*, from

1855, for a dime, or *Hymns for Children*, published in 1825, for fifty cents. Many times he took his books to the store on Bancroft Way owned by Harry Lawton, a young and enthusiastic aspiring writer who eventually became a good friend. Once in a while Grandpa got really lucky, like the time he stopped at Volunteer's, usually a barren place, just as they carried in three boxes of books and found a prize for a dime that he could turn around and sell for ten dollars. Most days he made two to five dollars, enough to buy some dinner and a little tobacco and still have some left over to buy a few more books.

Tom came over several times every week, slipping his parents cash whether he could afford it or not, playing chess with his father, reading and critiquing his stories. They appreciated the small "loans" they received from him, and the twenty dollars Pat sometimes mailed to them. Jack tried to help when he could, but with two babies in the house already, he and Ruth didn't have much to spare.

Things eventually improved. Mary received an on-again, off-again job at the Heinz Company, probably working in a cannery, where many times she had to wait for them to call her to come to work that day, but at least it was something. Grandpa was making a meager but steady income, enough to smoke a few cigarettes a day, keep the dog fed, buy some eggs, even meat once in a while. He started to get a name for himself as a rare book expert and made contacts in town among the owners of used bookstores. "I hear you know more about rare books than anyone in Berkeley," a new employee of the store told him once. Grandpa shrugged it off, but it must have pleased him secretly. In 1952 he got a job at Campus Textbooks, writing catalogs for their book inventories and occasionally minding the front of the store, which he hated. It was probably a good thing that he couldn't see the future, since in a few years his only job would be minding a store.

In August 1952 Grandpa received some the best news he'd

received in a couple of years: Macmillan was going to be sending him a royalty check for *Doc Dillahay* for approximately eight hundred dollars. He was ecstatic: "At long last I will be able to take a few breaths!"[20] When the check did arrive, however, it was soon spent on back rent and living expenses.

By 1953 Grandpa was writing plenty of stories. His agent was pleased with his production, although few, if any, were sold. He and Mary were carving out a small life for themselves in Berkeley, full of children and grandchildren, friends like Harry Lawton, bookstores, and the occasional movie or college football game. He was still struggling over drinking; the journal resonates worry about when he'll drink again, how much, and how he'll feel afterward.

Grandpa's journal ends in 1954. He had stopped writing every day by that point, and several weeks would often go by before he would write again. Stopping writing in the journal was a good sign; he had noticed that when his and Mary's lives were fuller, he wrote less in the journal.

He wrote stories in spurts; but most, if not all, of them were rejected. He eventually finished another manuscript, but with the name "The Strange Case of Christopher Sperm," one can only imagine what it was about. Grandpa sent it to Macmillan for consideration. They rejected it. Eventually, the manuscript was tossed or burned.

Grandpa had found a relatively stable life at Farrell's, probably the store with floor-to-ceiling chaos that I remember. Somehow, he and Mary managed.

Most of the documents in Grandpa's papers that date from 1958 on consist of letters from Jack. It was as if Grandpa and Mary's world became centered around whatever news they received from him. As 1960 and 1961 came and went, their front-row seats must have been terrifying.

In January 1963 they received the last letter from my father. By this time he had been admitted to sanitariums—one being Napa State Hospital—four times. Now he was in a hospital in Mendocino. The novelty of being in sanitariums had long ago worn off, as seen from the subdued tone of the following letter:

> Things are going along, according to routine here—I'm getting that "50 minute hour" of individual therapy, twice weekly, plus group therapy. I feel like I'm approaching the time when I can at least navigate out there. Will have to plan on prolonged therapy, however, soon.
>
> Since opportunities are so limited up here, I will probably migrate south again. As long as I can keep clear of Phyl the Pill and Demon Rum, I may make it.
>
> Your letters help more than you know.
>
> Love, Jack.
> P.S. A large, soft prostate is a helluva lot better than a small hard one. J.[21]

With the exception of one small letter, there is absolutely nothing in the boxes of my grandfather's papers dated after 1964, the year my father died. It is as if all communication with the outside world stopped at that point.

We might never have found out what happened to Grandpa if other relatives in the family hadn't prodded us to do the detective work. In 1979 our grandmother Velma—Grandpa's first wife—called Linda. Of all the relatives on the Powers side, Velma faithfully tended to her grandchildren. It was as if she felt she needed to compensate for the lack of attendance from her ex-husband and her son. But she always complained bitterly about her ex-husband.

But she was worried now. No one had heard from Grandpa or Mary in years.

My sisters and I hesitated. The memories were so painful,

especially for Linda. When she lived with Grandpa and Mary for a few months in 1966, they were living on the border of Berkeley and Oakland in a second-floor apartment. At that time he was well advanced in his alcoholism and rarely sober.

Finally, Linda and I decided to go down to the county offices in Oakland and see what we could find out. I hoped we wouldn't find anything. If we did, chances are it would only be bad news. But maybe we would get lucky; I hoped for the long shot, that we'd find out that Grandpa still worked at the bookstore, ready to hand out books as part of his grandfatherly duties.

The Vital Statistics room at the County Recorder was full of floor-to-ceiling shelves where mammoth books are stored that list the dates of births and deaths. The clerk directed us to the P's. Anticipating a long search, Linda and I settled down for a few hours of tedious reading. We opened up the first book.

"There it is," Linda said.

It was on the very first page. Powers, Paul S., Death: 1971. Last known address: Manila Street, Oakland.

I looked around the cavernous room and wished I hadn't come. I wanted to keep things as they were, so I could think that Grandpa was still there somewhere, conveniently waiting for me when I was brave enough to find him.

We asked for a copy of the death certificate. He had died on March 1, 1971, of a "subdural hematoma." At the bottom of the certificate the coroner had typed: "Head injury from unknown collapse or fall. Alcohol: Absent."

Mary had moved in with Pat after Grandpa died, yet she lived only one more year. She was always too upset over Grandpa's death, Pat said, to want to talk about the circumstances behind it, and Pat didn't want to press it. Mary had been Grandpa's closest friend and ally, and just like he had asked for in his memoir, she had been there until the last time the cover was dropped over the ol' typewriter.

19. Pat and Tom at the family reunion, 1999. *Author photo.*

A few weeks after meeting Pat, my mother and Linda and Becky flew down to southern California for a family reunion. We took advantage of an extra day beforehand and headed toward Laguna Beach. The Pacific Coast Highway gently undulates beside the ocean, and on the top of each hill you can see the water on your left, the orange and olive-green hills on your right, and an endless row of buildings bordering each side of the highway.

We stopped at a small ice cream shop and ordered sodas. My mother stared out the window at the roaring, endless din of traffic. How was it going to feel for her to see them tomorrow, I wondered. She had quietly stayed on the periphery through all of this, saying all the right things. "I'm so happy you found all this, Laurie." Saying it like she meant it. Never jealous. Always there to answer questions.

At Pat's front door, we smiled and hugged. We laughed, ate, took pictures, asked questions. We sat around Pat's backyard patio table and passed around the few issues of *Wild West Weekly* that Tom had kept, and marveled at the stories. We studied the remainder of Grandpa's rare book collection that filled the built-in bookcases in her living room and spilled into more bookcases lining one entire wall in the den.

I'd assumed that I would suddenly be overpowered by a rush of tears at the reunion. Oddly enough, I wasn't. Perhaps crying will come later, I thought, when all the years missed, the letters unwritten, the phone calls not made, the summers not spent together would rush at me, overwhelming me when I least expected it.

I nervously awaited my uncle Tom's arrival. He had always been the one I'd hoped to meet. After all, he was the closest thing to my father and grandfather. He could have been the surrogate patriarch when I grew up. Now that dream had evaporated. His senility had eventually been diagnosed as hydrocephalus, not Alzheimer's disease as Pat was originally told. He needed round-the-clock care; this excursion was only allowed because my aunt acted as a chauffeur, returning him to his care facility later. He was allowed to go for walks alone, something he loved. He departed for long, solitary walks, always returning to where he started.

Still, I had fantasies: he would suddenly open up to me

and begin talking about his father, his brother. Big secrets. Revelations. Answers to why things ended so sadly.

When he finally arrived, I immediately saw my father and my grandfather in his face, his glasses reminding me of the horn-rimmed glasses my father wore in later years.

"Remember Jack?" Pat asked him. "Your brother?" Tom's face didn't change. "This is Ruth, who was married to him," He politely smiled as he shook hands with my mother. "These are Jack's daughters," Pat continued. His blank look didn't change. He was obviously uncomfortable with these people he didn't remember.

"Oh," he said vaguely. He sat stiffly on a folding chair in front of the fireplace. Pat sat next to him, the interpreter. My sisters and I perched on the couch on the opposite side of the room, a trio of adoring fans.

He genially joined in the conversation and pleasantly answered our questions. Somehow the conversation turned to the 1960s, when he was in Europe. He answered agreeably: yes he had been there. He reeled off the names of several countries where he had lived. He remembers all of this, I thought, yet doesn't remember his father or his brother, his brilliant mind now darting between dark and light.

The conversation lagged, and Linda tried to remedy matters by asking Pat questions on an unrelated topic. Tom sat alone, mute, as the rest of the room chatted. Maybe it will help, I thought, if I show him pictures of George and Phyllis. Maybe they will jog his memory of his father. I knelt next to his chair, smelling the sweat from his walk that morning in the hot sun.

"Here, Tom, here are pictures of George."

"George?" He asked, looking at me coldly, appearing impatient, slightly annoyed.

"George, your father's brother?" I clarified. Was I being too condescending?

He looked at the picture of Phyllis. "That's his sister," I said.

"Then she's my father's sister also," he remarked.

"Yes," I said, excited that he made the connection. I flipped through a few more pictures for him.

He looked at his watch.

"Thank you very much," he abruptly said, not an act of gratitude, but an act of dismissal.

"Can I go now?" he asked his sister after being there fifteen minutes.

As he left, he politely said good-bye to my mother, as if saying good-bye to someone he had just met. She replied politely, trying to be casual and cordial, but her face fell in disappointment. Tom began to walk out the door, but he suddenly turned and looked at my mother again. "Good-bye, Ruth," he said. He walked toward her a few steps.

"Ruth," he repeated, holding his arms out for an embrace. My mother had tears in her eyes as they hugged. He turned away, then turned back again and raised his hand in a wave.

"It was good to see you again, Ruth."

Later that summer, Pat and I drove to the Autry Western Heritage Museum, an elegant building in Burbank, proudly announcing its dedication to the study of the West. One of Grandpa's Little Big Books, *Spook Riders on the Overland*, is at the museum.

For the most part, the world forgot about pulps. Most ended up in the trash bin, except those few collected by people for either sentimental reasons or investment. The companies disappeared along with invaluable collections of archives. Street & Smith, which resorted to publishing yearbooks in its later years and was eventually bought out by Condé Nast in 1961, didn't bother to protect their collection of pulp art. The new company put the remaining original pulp paintings out with the trash.[22]

Many people would say good riddance. The pulps choked with violence. Still, old fans and collectors have rallied around pulp fiction over the years. Cover art has certainly gained large numbers of collectors and admirers. Numerous anthologies of pulp stories have been collected over the years. After all, amid the mediocrity there were many, many good stories. The historical importance of pulp fiction magazines, for their place in popular culture and their influence on other literature, films, and art, has always been there—and rarely recognized.

Historians of pulp fiction have contributed numerous works over the years, and a respectable canon is growing. Unfortunately, many older books are heavy on anecdotal accounts, many of which have been proven to be inaccurate. For decades, a sturdy and steadfast group of collectors and enthusiasts throughout the country has studied the cultural phenomenon of pulp fiction. PulpCon, a convention celebrating the pulp magazine, is held every year.

The magazines are enjoying a healthy renaissance as a collector's item on internet auction sites. Strangely enough, issues of *Wild West Weekly* have been highly sought after over the past twenty years, more than *Western Story* and the other best-selling magazines. In 1983, John Dinan wrote: "*Wild West Weekly* has the distinction of being the only Western pulp magazine with a modern following. . . . [It] has, today, a hard core of devotees who collect and read these magazines with a passion born of a deep love for the Western yarn. The magazines are sold and traded via an underground that would do credit to the French Resistance Forces of World War II."[23] Judging from internet auction sites, this has not changed since Dinan's book was published.

As for my grandfather, he is mentioned in at least three books on pulp fiction, and several have mentioned Sonny Tabor and Kid Wolf as important figures of 1930s pulp Westerns. I have found no better tribute to Grandpa than the following by Redd Boggs in his essay "I Remember *Wild West Weekly*":

Undoubtedly among the chief factors in the popularity of the "new" www was the introduction of two new characters whose hard riding and straight shooting soon took the play away from the circle J Outfit. Kid Wolf and Sonny Tabor became by all odds the favorite characters of nearly all 3w readers, and they continued to appear with scarcely diminished popularity till the very end. . . . A prolific hack writer in the early days, he was able to grow with the magazine and hold his own among the somewhat more skillful scriveners who began to appear in the magazine in the 1940's. . . . Fittingly enough, the very last issue of the magazine (November, 1943) contained two Powers novelettes.[24]

When Pat and I arrived at the museum, a historian led us past the exhibit halls full of saddles, guns, and movie posters up to the second floor and to the special collections exhibit. She brought out *Spook Riders on the Overland,* and Pat held it in her hand. I snapped a picture of her holding the book.

While Pat browsed through the other books, I wandered over to the bookshelves that held hundreds of books on Western history and memorabilia. One book looked interesting: a bibliography of Big Little Books and similar publications. It had a section listed by author. I flipped to that section, and the pictures and the names brought me back to that day in the Smith library. So much had happened, so much had been uncovered since that first day. There was nothing else to find, I was sure.

I found *Spook Riders, Buckskin and Bullets,* and *Johnny Forty-five.* All were listed next to illustrations of their covers.

But I had to look again.

I couldn't believe it. There was a title I had never seen before.

Desert Justice, by Ward M. Stevens.

AFTERWORD

For the most part, my grandfather's memoir correctly correlates with the history of *Wild West Weekly* and the progression of events at Street & Smith. Grandpa left out a lot of his personal life, and he barely mentioned the biggest struggle of his life, alcoholism. In his defense, the intent of *Pulp Writer* is clear: it is about the pulp fiction industry, not his personal demons. There are a few omissions, however, that merit discussion here.

One is the shooting incident I learned about from the documents I received from Lillie Whiteman early in my search. The incident that was reported in the *Rice County Monitor* in 1920, in which my grandfather was reported as "doing nicely," was never mentioned in the memoir. This is curious considering that, according to a 1949 interview for *Doc Dillahay* publicity, the incident resulted from his desire to be an "authentic" Western writer. Eager to get the feel for how a gunslinger really twirls his guns, Grandpa borrowed one of his father's revolvers, took it out to the backyard, and started pistol-whipping in the "approved movie-cowboy manner." He promptly shot himself in the chest.

But my aunt remembers her mother saying it was a suicide attempt. No one else in the family recalls this story. What actually happened and why Grandpa didn't include it in the memoir remain a mystery. Maybe it really was a bungled attempt at fancy-finger work and he was too embarrassed to write about it. But considering his ease in poking fun at himself in the rest of the memoir, this doesn't make sense.

Grandpa also mentions his feelings of separateness when living in Little River. He was treated like an outcast, he says.

His half brother, George, however, remembers the town fondly and recollects the respect and love that the town felt toward Dr. Powers and his family.

My grandfather does not mention a brief stint in the navy when he was sixteen. Without his father's consent, he ran off, lied about his age, and enlisted. It didn't last. His father managed to get him out, but not before Grandpa got the obligatory tattoo.

Grandpa limits the discussion of his first wife, my father's mother, to a few lines. Velma Niccum was a vivacious dark-haired beauty from Black Hawk who was as outspoken as Grandpa was quiet. Theirs was an obvious case of opposites attracting, but the relationship was short-lived and volatile from the start. Velma became pregnant with my father, Jack, almost immediately. After the couple moved back to Black Hawk, she began to attract the attention of other men. According to George, the sheriff of Black Hawk began to "make eyes" at her, and Paul, full of ghost towns and stories of the West, threatened to shoot him. Paul's father, however, intervened and talked Paul into giving him the gun.

Although George and Phyllis seem to have escaped the ravages of alcoholism that eventually conquered their brother, Grandpa's full sister, Nell, did not. Nell was beautiful, according to Phyllis, and photographs of her attest to that. But she married badly—at least three times—and drank. After Grandpa's death, George and Phyllis kept in touch with Nell, who lived most of her life in the San Diego area. She died in 1981.

My uncle Tom died in the summer of 2005. He died of pneumonia, although his mental capacities had never improved since the original diagnosis of hydrocephalus. Still, he enjoyed some quality of life in the last years; with his caretaker he traveled to Hawaii, San Francisco, and Mexico.

I enjoy spending time with my aunt Pat. We have spent a good deal of time together, and I moved to the Los Angeles area in 2006 partly to be able to spend more time with her and her children, my cousins. My hopes of having a relationship with my uncle were gone, but this friendship with Pat has turned into more than a one-summer reunion.

I respect my grandfather—and his work—much more now. His ability to pound out twelve-thousand-word stories week in and week out, stories that continually were funny, fast-moving, and colorful, still astounds me. He was a gifted writer who was able to polish his craft in the pulps and then use it to his best advantage to write a truly entertaining novel.

ACKNOWLEDGMENTS

I'm sure my grandfather would have loved to acknowledge many people, especially those he loved. Unfortunately, he is not here to do so, but he does write about many of those who helped him within the pages of his book.

I would like to thank those who helped me in the research for the biographical essays. My aunt Pat Binkley and her husband, Ted, have been exceedingly generous with my grandfather's personal papers and their collection of *Wild West Weekly* magazines.

This book began as an honors thesis while I was a student at Smith College. My thesis adviser, Daniel Horowitz, was there from the very beginning and encouraged me to start research, even though I had serious doubts that I would find anything at all. For your unshakable faith in this project, I thank you, Dan.

My agent, Jon Tuska, offered his invaluable experience as both a Western historian and a pulp fiction expert. He was there to talk about pulp fiction, Westerns, and literary history, a rarity in this world. He was one of the few people I could talk shop with. All of this helped me turn out a book that I know my grandfather would have been proud of.

Ann Parker gently pushed me to start writing again after I had completely given up and buried this book once and for all. Ann would have none of that, however, and her insistence that we meet on a regular basis with completed pages to critique resurrected this project from the ashes.

My cousin Maureen and my aunt Pat painstakingly typed the original *Pulp Writer* into an electronic file, something far beyond what a writer's relatives should ever have to do. My mother and my sisters Linda and Becky were always there for me when I bothered them for their memories, even after the novelty of this project wore off.

Jim Adams of Berkeley opened a door into the little-known history of book collecting in 1950s Berkeley and Oakland with one little phone call. Lillie Whiteman, Dorothy Goodrick, Howard Hodgson, and Ruth Perry of Little River, Kansas, told me stories and mailed me materials that were instrumental in discovering the history of my grandfather's early life. Randolph Cox of the *Dime Novel Roundup* provided me with valuable facts and sources. Steven Somers and Duane Powers took the time to send me e-mails that changed my life forever. The staff at Syracuse University Library was especially helpful and patient.

I want to thank my great–uncle George Powers and his family, Sheri Ann Dante, Sherry Emmons, Marilyn Russell, Jennifer White, Kimberly Marlowe, Ken Kurtis, Brian Bodtker, and Kris and Sara Feldman.

And finally, I want to thank Larry Estep, who compiled a complete list of *Wild West Weekly* issues—listing the story titles and the authors cross-referenced with their pseudonyms for the period from 1928 to 1943—onto a CD-ROM. His amazing patience in listing such an incredible amount of detail saved me untold amounts of time and eliminated the need for me to take a second trip to Syracuse to the Street & Smith archives.

NOTES

DISCOVERING *PULP WRITER*

1. Powers, *Doc Dillahay*, 3.
2. Stevens [Powers], *Wanted—Sonny Tabor*, 88.
3. Stevens [Powers], *Wanted—Sonny Tabor*, 13.
4. Stevens [Powers], *Wanted—Sonny Tabor*, 33.
5. "Little River, Kansas," http://www.skyways.org/towns/Lit tleRiver/index.html.
6. "Sixty Years Ago," *Rice County Monitor Journal*, June 24, 1960.
7. Dinan, *The Pulp Western*, 5, 6.
8. Street & Smith bookkeeping document, June 1940, Street & Smith Archives, Syracuse University Library, Syracuse, New York.
9. Johannsen, *The House of Beadle and Adams*.
10. Reynolds, *The Fiction Factory*, 38.
11. Goodstone, *The Pulps*, xii.
12. Goulart, *Cheap Thrills*, 12.
13. An Old Scout, "Young Wild West's Prairie Pioneers; Or, Fighting the Way to the Golden Loop," *Wild West Weekly*, May 6, 1904, 9.
14. Reynolds, *The Fiction Factory*, 154.
15. Reynolds, *The Fiction Factory*, 156.
16. Reynolds, *The Fiction Factory*, 157.
17. Ward M. Stevens [Paul S. Powers], "The Gunman of Monterey," *Wild West Weekly*, November 3, 1928, 78.
18. Stevens [Powers], "The Gunman of Monterey," 84.
19. Andrew A. Griffin [Paul S. Powers], "The Fightin' Poet," *Wild West Weekly*, July 20, 1929, 114.
20. Andrew A. Griffin [Paul S. Powers], "Hog Legs for Range Hogs," *Wild West Weekly*, November 1943, 49.
21. Ward M. Stevens [Paul S. Powers], "Smoky Round-up on the Overland," *Wild West Weekly*, December 18, 1937, 59, 61.

22. Walker Tompkins, "The Oklahoma Kid's Rancho Visit," *Wild West Weekly*, July 9, 1938, 11.

23. Ward M. Stevens [Paul S. Powers], "Turkeys and Buzzards for Kid Wolf," *Wild West Weekly*, November 30, 1935, 16–17.

24. Ward M. Stevens [Paul S. Powers], "Sonny Tabor and the Devil's Posse," *Wild West Weekly*, October 10, 1931, 11–12.

25. Chuck Martin, "The Devil's Calling Card," *Wild West Weekly*, June 15, 1940, 18.

26. Cleve Endicott [Ronald Oliphant], "Thanksgivin' in Hard Luck Hollow," *Wild West Weekly*, November 30, 1935, 79.

27. Ward M. Stevens [Paul S. Powers], "Sonny Tabor's Errand of Justice," *Wild West Weekly*, July 14, 1934, 32.

28. Ward M. Stevens [Paul S. Powers], "Law Guns for Sonny Tabor's Christmas," *Wild West Weekly*, December 26, 1936, 30.

29. Estep, *Index*.

30. Estep, *Index*.

31. Pronzini, *Six-Gun in Cheek*, 42.

32. Bud the Kid, "Wrangler's Corner," *Wild West Weekly*, November 21, 1936, 126.

33. Bob Stratton to Paul Powers, December 27, 1940, Paul Powers papers, private collection.

34. Henry E. Ralston to "Esther," March 17, 1957, Street & Smith Archives.

35. Ronald Oliphant to Paul Powers, January 16, 1934, Powers papers.

36. Patricia Binkley, interview by the author, June 13, 1999, Powers papers.

37. Ronald Oliphant to Paul Powers, March 25, 1938, Powers papers.

1. I'D WRITE A MILE

1. Willets, *Workers of the Nation*, 918–19.

2. Willets, *Workers of the Nation*, 920–21.

3. Willets, *Workers of the Nation*, 917, 924.

4. FOR WHOM THE BELLBOY TOILS

1. Halsey, *Authors of Our Day*, 271.

6. AD ASTRA PER ASPERA, ADD ASPIRIN

1. Although it can be argued that Street & Smith was, at the time of the writing of *Pulp Writer*, the oldest *surviving* pulp publisher, it was not the first to publish pulp fiction magazines. Beadle and Adams published dime novels before Street & Smith, and Frank Munsey published the first pulp fiction magazine, *Argosy*, in 1896, long before Street & Smith transitioned from dime novels to pulp magazines. See "Discovering *Pulp Writer*" in this volume for details.

10. TRICKS OF THE TRADE

1. No letter in the Powers papers has been found that contains these exact words. However a November 19, 1928, letter from Ronald Oliphant to Paul Powers begins, "I was glad to receive your novelette 'THE TROUBLE DODGER FROM DODGE.' I will purchase this story this week, but I do think it shows a tendency to pack in too much action. It is something like a moving picture that is running too fast so that the effect is somewhat spoiled. Very often it is better to take a little slower pace and work up to a good climax than to overcrowd your story with exciting incidents piling them one on top of another."

2. Ronald Oliphant to Paul Powers, December 16, 1929, Powers papers.

3. Ronald Oliphant to Paul Powers, February 18, 1935, Powers papers.

4. Ronald Oliphant to Paul Powers, November 19, 1934, Powers papers.

5. Ronald Oliphant to Paul Powers, December 15, 1937, Powers papers.

6. Ronald Oliphant to Paul Powers, May 29, 1931, Powers papers.

7. Ronald Oliphant to Paul Powers, August 30, 1935, Powers papers.

8. Ronald Oliphant to Paul Powers, April 13, 1931, Powers papers.

9. Ronald Oliphant to Paul Powers, June 30, 1932, Powers papers.

10. Ronald Oliphant to Paul Powers, December 21, 1936, Powers papers.
11. Ronald Oliphant to Paul Powers, March 30, 1934, Powers papers.
12. Ronald Oliphant to Paul Powers, May 8, 1933, Powers papers.
13. Ronald Oliphant to Paul Powers, January 18, 1934, Powers papers.
14. Ronald Oliphant to Paul Powers, April 28, 1936, Powers papers.
15. Ronald Oliphant to Paul Powers, August 27, 1928, Powers papers.
16. Ronald Oliphant to Paul Powers, date unknown.
17. Ronald Oliphant to Paul Powers, March 22, 1930, Powers papers.
18. Ferguson, *Mark Twain*, chapter 13.

11. TUMBLEWEED IN ARIZONA

1. E. S. Robinson, *Practical Psychology*, 419.

LIFE AFTER THE PULPS

1. Ronald Oliphant to Paul Powers, September 6, 1934, Powers papers.
2. Francis L. Stebbins to Paul Powers, May 8, 1940, Powers papers.
3. James P. Webb, "Pilgrim on the Prod," *Wild West Weekly*, August 30, 1941, 16.
4. John Burr to Paul Powers, July 24, 1941, Powers papers.
5. John Burr to Paul Powers, February 18, 1942, Powers papers.
6. Delbert Ganns, "Reader's Branding Irons," *Wild West Weekly*, August 2, 1941, 112.
7. Howard Lassen, "Reader's Branding Irons," *Wild West Weekly*, August 30, 1941, 113.
8. Jack Powers, "Reader's Branding Irons," *Wild West Weekly*, January 31, 1942, 113.
9. John Burr to Paul Powers, May 13, 1943, Powers papers.
10. John Burr to Paul Powers, July 20, 1943, Powers papers.

11. Griffin [Powers], "Hog Legs for Range Hogs," *Wild West Weekly*, November 1943, 58.

12. Editorial note, "Death Blots the Brands," *Wild West Weekly*, November 1943, 29.

13. Chuck Martin to Paul Powers, October 28, 1949, Powers papers.

14. Lisle Bell, review of *Doc Dillahay*, by Paul S. Powers, *New York Herald Tribune Weekly Book Review*, March 6, 1949, 12; Paul Jordan Smith, "I'll Be Judge, You Be Jury," *Los Angeles Times*, May 22, 1949.

15. Hoffman Birney, review of *Doc Dillahay*, by Paul S. Powers, *New York Times Book Review*, March 13, 1949, 22.

16. Eleanor Daniels to Paul Powers, July 17, 1950, Powers papers.

17. Eleanor Daniels to Paul Powers, October 13, 1950, Powers papers.

18. Paul S. Powers, unpublished journal, June 9, 1951, Powers papers.

19. Powers, journal, June 9, 1951.

20. Powers, journal, August 1, 1952.

21. Jack Powers to Paul S. Powers, January 3, 1963, Powers papers.

22. Doug Stewart, "Guys and Molls," *Smithsonian Magazine*, August 2003, 58.

23. Dinan, *The Pulp Western*, 16.

24. Boggs, "I Remember *Wild West Weekly*," 21–22.

BIBLIOGRAPHY

Allen, Frederick Lewis. *Only Yesterday and Since Yesterday: A Popular History of the '20s and '30s.* New York: Bonanza Books, 1986. Reprint of *Only Yesterday* (Harper & Row, 1931) and *Since Yesterday* (Harper & Brothers, 1931).

Boggs, Redd. "I Remember *Wild West Weekly.*" In John Dinan, *The Pulp Western: A Popular History of the Western Fiction Magazine in America,* 17–33. San Bernardino CA: Borgo Press, 1983.

Carr, Nick. *The Western Pulp Hero: An Investigation into the Psyche of an American Legend.* Mercer Island WA: Starmont House, 1989.

Cawelti, John. *The Six Gun Mystique Sequel.* Bowling Green OH: Bowling Green State University Press, 1999.

Cooper, James Fenimore. *The Last of the Mohicans.* 1826. New York: Fine Creative Media, 2003.

Cox, Randolph. "Our Popular Publishers: Number One: Frank Tousey." *Dime Novel Roundup,* August 1994, 72–73.

Dinan, John. *The Pulp Western: A Popular History of the Western Fiction Magazine in America.* San Bernardino CA: Borgo Press, 1983.

Estep, Larry. *An Index to Wild West Weekly.* Compact disc. Morehead KY, 2001.

Ferguson, John DeLancey. *Mark Twain: Man and Legend.* Indianapolis: Bobbs-Merrill, 1943.

Goodstone, Tony. *The Pulps: Fifty Years of American Pop Culture.* New York: Chelsea House, 1970.

Goulart, Ron. *Cheap Thrills: An Informal History of the Pulp Magazines.* New Rochelle NY: Arlington House, 1972.

Griffin, Andrew A. [Paul S. Powers]. *Johnny Forty-five.* Akron OH: Saalfield, 1939.

Gruber, Frank. *The Pulp Jungle.* Los Angeles: Sherbourne Press, 1967.

Halsey, Francis Whiting. *Authors of Our Day in Their Homes.* New York: James Pott, 1902.

Hersey, Harold. *The New Pulpwood Editor.* 1937. Reprint, Silver Spring MD: Adventure House, 2002.

Johannsen, Albert. *The House of Beadle and Adams.* Norman: University of Oklahoma Press, 1950. http://www.niulib.niu.edu/badndp/bibindex.html.

Kennedy, David M. *Freedom from Fear: The American People in Depression and War: 1929–1945.* New York: Oxford University Press, 1999.

Lowery, Lawrence F. *Lowery's: The Collector's Guide to Big Little Books and Similar Books.* Danville CA: Educational Research and Applications Corporation, 1981.

McElvaine, Robert S. *The Great Depression.* New York: Times Books, 1984.

Powers, Paul S. *Doc Dillahay.* New York: Macmillan, 1949.

Pronzini, Bill. *Six-Gun in Cheek.* Minneapolis: Crossover Press, 1997.

———, ed. *Wild Westerns: Stories from the Grand Old Pulps.* New York: Walker, 1986.

Reynolds, Quentin. *The Fiction Factory; Or, From Pulp Row to Quality Street.* New York: Random House, 1955.

Robinson, Edward S. *Practical Psychology.* 1929. Reprint, New York: Macmillan, 1934.

Robinson, Frank M., and Lawrence Davidson. *Pulp Culture: The Art of Fiction Magazines.* Portland: Collector's Press, 1998.

Server, Lee. *Danger Is My Business.* San Francisco: Chronicle Books, 1993.

———. *Encyclopedia of Pulp Fiction Writers.* New York: Checkmark Books, 2002.

Smith, Erin A. *Hard-boiled: Working-Class Readers and Pulp Magazines.* Philadelphia: Temple University Press, 2000.

Smith, Henry Nash. *Virgin Land: The American West as Symbol and Myth.* 2nd ed. Cambridge: Harvard University Press, 1978.

Springhall, John. "The Dime Novel as Scapegoat for Juvenile Crime: Anthony Comstock's Campaign to Suppress the 'Half-Dime' Western of the 1880s." *Dime Novel Roundup,* August 1994, 63–72.

Stevens, Ward M. [Paul S. Powers]. *Kid Wolf of Texas: A Western Story.* New York: Chelsea House, 1930.

———. *The Ranger and the Cowboy: A Sonny Tabor Story.* Akron OH: Saalfield, 1939.

———. *Spook Riders on the Overland: A Freckles Malone Story.* Akron OH: Saalfield, 1939.

———. *Wanted—Sonny Tabor: A Western Story.* New York: Chelsea House, 1931.

Stewart, Doug. "Guys and Molls." *Smithsonian Magazine*, August 2003, 54–58.

Tuska, Jon, ed. *The Big Book of Western Action Stories.* Edison NJ: Castle Books, 2000.

Willets, Gilson. *Workers of the Nation.* New York: Collier, 1903.

Wister, Owen. *The Virginian.* New York: Macmillan, 1902.

INDEX